What to Do
When the Roof
Caves In

WHAT TO DO
WHEN THE ROOF
CAVES IN

BY MARILYN MEBERG

THOMAS NELSON
Since 1798

NASHVILLE   DALLAS   MEXICO CITY   RIO DE JANEIRO   BEIJING

Published in Nashville, Tennessee, by Thomas Nelson. Thomas Nelson is a registered trademark of Thomas Nelson, Inc.

Thomas Nelson, Inc., titles may be purchased in bulk for educational, business, fund-raising, or sales promotional use. For information, please e-mail SpecialMarkets@ThomasNelson.com.

Unless otherwise noted, all Scripture references are taken from the *Holy Bible*, New Living Translation. © 1996. Used by permission of Tyndale House Publishers, Inc., Wheaton, Illinois 60189. All rights reserved.

Scripture references marked GNT are taken from THE GOOD NEWS TRANSLATION. © 1976, 1992 by The American Bible Society. Used by permission. All rights reserved.

Scripture references marked KJV are taken from the King James Version of the Bible.

Scripture references marked MSG are taken from *The Message* by Eugene H. Peterson. © 1993, 1994, 1995, 1996, 2000. Used by permission of NavPress Publishing Group. All rights reserved.

Scripture references marked NASB are taken from the NEW AMERICAN STANDARD BIBLE®. © The Lockman Foundation 1960, 1962, 1963, 1968, 1971, 1972, 1973, 1975, 1977, 1995. Used by permission.

Scripture references marked NIV are taken from the HOLY BIBLE: NEW INTERNATIONAL VERSION®. © 1973, 1978, 1984 by International Bible Society. Used by permission of Zondervan Publishing House. All rights reserved.

Scripture references marked NKJV are taken from THE NEW KING JAMES VERSION. © 1982 by Thomas Nelson, Inc. Used by permission. All rights reserved.

Library of Congress Cataloging-in-Publication Data

Meberg, Marilyn.
    What to do when the roof caves in : woman-to-woman advice for tackling life's trials / by Marilyn Meberg.
      p. cm.
    ISBN 978-1-4002-0246-1
    1. Christian women—Religious life. 2. Problem solving—Religious aspects—Christianity. 3. Crisis management—Religious aspects—Christianity. I. Title.
BV4527.M437 2009
248.8'6082—dc22   2008049386

Printed in the United States of America

09 10 11 12 13 QW 6 5 4

CONTENTS

v

CONTENTS

1

SOLUTIONS AND CAVE-INS

D on't you love to hear the words, "I've got just the solution for your problem"? The word *solution* is full of promise; it lifts my spirit and renews my hope.

The problem I'm about to describe to you is admittedly not high on the scale of big-bigger-biggest, but it nevertheless was one for which I wanted a solution. And incidentally, any solution that comes packed with a few giggles is my favorite kind. So let me share it with you—who knows, maybe you've been looking for a solution for this very same problem.

Each spring I plant a gorgeous garden of flowers: petunias, snapdragons, and pansies (to name a few). I love my flowers. The problem is, so do the Texas neighborhood wild rabbits that appear out of nowhere! Shortly after my plantings (in each of the three years I've lived in Texas), the ravenous and relentless appetites of multiple rabbit families descend upon my garden and eat each little plant right down to the nubbins. Then they have the audacity to stand outside my window mouthing the words, "We're still hungry." So like any conscientious moron, I replant. Like any brilliant rabbit family who knows a moron when they see one, they again descend upon my new plantings, reducing them to "nubness." For years I have been in need of a solution for my victimization.

Three weeks ago it happened: the solution. I was getting a haircut and complaining about the high cost of keeping the neighborhood rabbits fed. One of the women having a root touch-up turned from her magazine and said "I can tell you exactly how to get rid of your rabbits—human hair. They are repulsed by human hair. All you have to do is spread hair around the roots of your flowers. I promise they will flee."

I looked at Natalie who was cutting my hair. It was 3:15 in the afternoon, so her wastebasket contained a day's worth of hair. She stopped cutting, stared at me a moment, and then said, "You want it?" It seemed like such a "hairbrained" idea, but I loved the quirkiness of it—and of course, I was desperate. "Yeah, I really want it!" She grabbed a Wal-Mart bag out of her cupboard, dumped the hair supply into it, and within seconds I sailed out the door with a bag of rabbit solution.

On the way home I started thinking about when I should do the hair sprinkling. I felt self-conscious about being seen crawling through my garden sifting wisps of hair around. I decided to wait until eight o'clock p.m. when I could do my work under the cover of approaching nightfall.

When I felt I had sufficient twilight, I started hairing up my backyard flower beds. I was surprised to find I soon lost enthusiasm for the project: my back hurt, my fingers lost "nimbility," and the hair gave me the creeps. There was brown hair, black hair, blonde hair, grey hair (mine), and multicolored hair starting at the roots. By the time I reached the front yard I was eager to be finished and was no longer sifting the hair. I was dropping it about in clumps, which could be mistaken for poorly maintained little toupees.

I was nearly finished when a car approached my house going very slowly. I did not want to turn around . . . I did not want to be recognized. I continued dropping hair clumps. The car then pulled into my driveway. With the motor still running I heard the window lower and the familiar voice of my friend Luci Swindoll. Her words:

"What in the world are you doing? I drove over here to see why you are not answering your phone, and I see you hunkered down among your flowers with a Wal-Mart bag in your left hand, a rubber glove on your right hand, and you're tossing something about."

I rose up to my full height and told her what I'd learned about a rabbit solution (she too is plagued with hungry rabbits) and that I had a day's hair supply given to me by Natalie when I got my hair cut that afternoon.

She stared wordlessly at me for at least a full minute. I figured she was thinking maybe the idea made sense and perhaps she'd better try it too. Instead, she leaned out the window and in a loud conspiratorial whisper said, "Marilyn, do you realize you are spreading the DNA of perfect strangers all over your property? I'm sure that's not even moral! And not only that, what do you think the neighbors are thinking? You look as if you're trying to destroy evidence from a crime scene!"

I accused her of watching too many episodes of *CSI*, but I took her up on the offer to go get a soy chai tea latte. Until that moment, it had not been a pleasant evening.

So here's the proof the solution works: I have no more rabbits! I think they all scooted immediately over to Luci's property where there continues to be good eating. What puzzles me, though, is that Luci refuses my hair solution. I got a new hairbag yesterday, which I offered to share. She says she cannot accept my offer because it would compromise her moral standards. Uh-huh!

Now this book is committed to providing solutions for problems far more serious than a band of marauding rabbits. Nevertheless, in a serious cave-in there may be a solution we'd never have considered simply because it falls under the category of "hairbrained."

In all reverence, I think many of God's solutions seem hairbrained. To name a few: How about Jonah being swallowed by a whale and left in its belly until Jonah repents of his disobedience? That confession is celebrated by the most significant vomit session in human history. Or the drama of the walls of Jericho, which crashed after a divinely synchronized yell from the Israelites. And then there's God's beloved prophet Hosea who was instructed to go out and find a wife; the one requirement for that wife was she must be a prostitute.

These seemingly hairbrained directives from God get my

attention, delight my soul, and upon careful study inspire my faith. They also inspire me to think outside the box regarding a search for cave-in solutions.

I'm totally committed to the reality that many of our cave-in solutions lie in the realm of how we think about them. I need to determine if what looks and feels like a cave-in really is one or is merely the presence of pesky rabbits. We need to avoid "awful-izing" what is happening to us. That's best accomplished by levelheaded thinking. What we think can totally skew reality.

Let me give you an example of how our thinking can be totally out of step with reality. You may be familiar with the name Joshua Bell; he is one of the world's finest violinists. In 2007 at the L'Enfant Plaza subway station in Washington DC, Bell took out his $3.5 million Stradivarius and began to play Bach's sonatas. He was dressed in jeans and wearing a baseball cap. Of the more than one thousand people who walked by, very few paid any attention. Mr. Bell regularly performs to sold-out audiences in the world's best concert halls. Why did Bell not draw a crowd at the subway? Here's why: He was neither dressed in formal attire, nor was he standing on a stage. He looked like any other subway performer playing for free. Of course he didn't sound like a subway performer, but that reality was not great enough to cause people to change their preconceived ideas and realize the music they were hearing was that of a virtuoso. Unbeknownst to the subway people, Bell was in fact participating in an undercover field study conducted by the *Washington Post*.

This seemingly hairbrained study illustrates how resistant most people are to thinking outside the box. "If you're wearing jeans and a ball cap and playing a violin in the subway station, there's no way you can be a virtuoso." So goes the thinking of many of us small-boxers.

On the other hand, we need to exercise the power of reason as we do our cave-in consideration. It is not beyond reason to extend our mental borders to include creative improbabilities. But it is totally beyond reason to insist something is good when it is obviously bad, or to insist something is safe when it is obviously life threatening.

Do you remember the Crandall Canyon Mine that tragically collapsed in 2007? The mine's roof collapsed with so much force it registered 3.9 on the Richter scale. The miners were trapped one thousand feet underground. Against the backdrop of the seemingly hopeless rescue efforts, the co-owner of the mine insisted it was safe. He wanted the public to think it was. But it wasn't. Six coal miners and three rescuers died in that cave-in.

The tragic reality of what happened in that mine is now on public record. One report detailed numerous safety violations had been reported to the owners of the mine, but they continued to extract coal. Among other things, the mine owners failed to report three previous collapses that could have tipped regulators off and prevented the tragedy. The mine design was so flawed it seemed destined for collapse. In other words, sound judgment and reason could have prevented that cave-in.

One of the greatest assaults to our thinking and believing is dealing with calamities. We tend to think Christians should not experience calamitous cave-ins. We believe that because we have put our faith in God, He will steer bad things away from us. Now of course we allow for little calamities like a root canal, a ding in the fender from a light pole that was not there yesterday, bad weather during a much-anticipated vacation, or not eating tomatoes because of the risk of salmonella. (As of this writing, they've determined it's not the tomatoes, but jalapeño peppers.)

But when the big stuff hits, like earthquakes, devastating floods, fires, tornadoes, and hurricanes, we think maybe God is indifferent to the suffering of His creation, for whom

He professes profound love. We ask "What is he doing? Has he simply turned his back and no longer sees what's happening?" It doesn't help when the language of the media and insurance companies categorizes those events as acts of God.

Now as you can see from the table of contents, this book is committed to providing some solutions for problems far more serious than a band of marauding rabbits. Nevertheless, in our heavier cave-ins there may be a solution we never would have considered simply because it falls under the category of "hairbrained."

I'm also committed to the reality that for many of life's problems we can find solutions by paying attention to how we think about these problems. Our thinking may not make the problem disappear, but it can change how we respond to it—the degree to which we feel defeated by it.

Equally important to how we think is what we believe. Sometimes it's hard to know if my reaction to a problem is based on what I think or what I believe. So for the sake of clarity, let's define the two words as I'm using them. To *think* is to exercise the power of human reason even as it considers the improbable. To *believe* is to have faith, confidence, and trust in God's sovereign intent.

So what causes the roofs of our lives to cave in? To answer

that question we need to do a roof exam. In so doing, we may find some roofs are so poorly constructed they are unable to withstand more than a slight breeze. Other roofs are sturdy, well constructed, and have withstood many storms without even losing a shingle. So why are some roofs strong and others weak? It's all in the construction.

The construction of our roofs involves what we think, what we believe, and then what we do about what we think and believe. If we're unwise in any of those three building components we will be in vulnerable positions preceding a cave-in.

I really do think it's possible to avoid many cave-ins, but the tragic reality is there are some cave-ins too great for any roof to withstand. In those cases we can find ourselves flattened by a tsunami-like storm we never saw coming. Not only did we not see it coming, we can't imagine why it struck us. It is at this point that our thinking and believing can get out of whack. Questions like, "Why did God let this happen to me?" "Am I being punished for something?" "I'm not sure I feel safe with God anymore." "Did He allow this or did He send this?"

When we find ourselves thinking and believing God doesn't care, doesn't intervene on our behalf, or simply leaves us alone to work things out, we need to do a roof repair. The purpose of the roof is to provide shelter and security from life-storms. If we're flattened by a cave-in, we can decide whether or not we want to pull ourselves out from beneath the rubble or curl up and simply lie there hoping to die.

Now I have to tell you I've had a few calamitous cave-ins where I had to seriously think whether pulling out from under the rubble was worth the effort. I was flattened, my faith shaken, and the promise that God has all things under His loving control did not ring true to my ears. I knew it was in Scripture but I lost the knowing it was in my life. My roof had totally blown off. What does that mean? It means how I thought about God and what I believed about God were altered.

I understand the devastation of death and saying good-bye to those I love. Those were huge losses to me but were nevertheless a part of the expected life cycle. I did not question what God was doing. I grieved what I was feeling. But when my daughter was raped at the age of seventeen and her virginity was wrenched from her, I had a cave-in that still shakes my roof. I had to do major roof repair.

So how did I repair my roof? My thinking and believing needed disaster repair. I chose in my thinking to believe. Believe what? Psalm 93:1 says, "The world is firmly established;

it cannot be moved" (NIV). Though the world felt shaken, I chose to believe that God keeps it firmly established. I cannot expect God to become a servant of my will. My will is that nothing bad will ever happen to me and to those I love. My will is that the world is so firmly established no shingles fly off my roof. God's will is that I trust Him even with the rape of my daughter. That repaired thinking did not come easily or quickly. But even more challenged from the experience was my belief system. I couldn't help but think, *How could God let such an awful thing happen?*

Since I define belief as faith, confidence, and trust in God's sovereign intent, I found the phrase "sovereign intent" the most difficult to repair. Surely that rape was not a part of God's sovereign intent. Didn't that rape spring from the depths of the sin-saturated world in which we live? I wasn't sure how to repair the damage done to my belief system. I don't know that I am ever going to fully understand evil and why it hits some, skips others, or totally buries a few.

But here's what I do know: When Adam and Eve disobeyed God, the universe fell under the weight of that sin. We have lived under the rubble of that massive cave-in ever since. Even so, God has a sovereign intent for every personal cave-in we experience—the big ones, the medium-sized ones, and the little wild rabbit ones. We were meant to live in a world devoid of all cave-ins.

God did not "will" rape, war, disease, injustice, murder, molestation, or any of the other calamities that fall upon us. To sin was a human choice. God allowed the choice. But now, as we sit in the disastrous consequence of that choice, God promises to bring good out of bad. That is God's sovereign intent.

In the last chapter of this book we will discuss how God plans to give His creation a second chance at the perfection that was lost in Eden. He will make a new earth . . . good creation will be restored. These are fascinating contempla tions. However, as we live in the here and now, I want to share with you one of my favorite roof repair verses. That verse is Isaiah 45:3. It helps me reconstruct my belief system:

> I will give you the treasure of darkness and hidden wealth of secret places. (NASB) ·

In the darkness of my cave-ins, I could not imagine I would find God-ordained treasures. It was not possible to see them in the hurt, confused, and resentful aftermath I experienced after Beth's rape. I began to see the treasures for my soul that came with forgiveness, compassion, and empathy. I was led to the "hidden wealth of secret places," which enabled me to think and believe God will give meaning to this evil experience—meaning not only for now but for the future.

Through the years I have become increasingly aware that "hidden wealth" has to do with soul enrichment. That wealth is not easily seen simply because it is hidden—it is waiting to be discovered in the dark places of our cave-ins. Those discoveries of wealth for our minds and souls reveal to us the abundant love of God. That love is never obliterated by circumstance. That love is never withdrawn when we whimper in the rubble of the unexpected, the unexplained, and the unwelcome.

Like any other human being on the earth who prefers a life of ease, stability, and perfection, I would never deliberately choose a cave-in. It comforts me some cave-ins can be avoided simply by using good sense. But since I don't always use good sense, the cave-in comes and I blame myself with words like, "Mercy, Marilyn . . . don't you know better? What's wrong with you?" So I have to get my roof repair going and vow to use better sense next time.

But for those times when good sense does not help and I'm in the eye of a storm that then crashes my roof, I remember the promise of God's sovereign intent. He will provide soul wealth, which gives the experience personal meaning.

In the following chapters we'll discuss how to duck a cave-in and what to do when you don't or can't. Some of these chapters will deal with the superserious and some will deal with the stuff that drives us crazy and we find ourselves rooting for "his or her" roof to cave in. (We're not always nice people who continually wish the best for others . . . well, OK . . . *I'm* not.) Just know there's always a solution!

Roof Maintenance

1. Tell about a time you needed a solution for a crazy problem. Was it a crazy solution?

2. Is it hard for you to think "outside the box"? Can you tell about a time when an out-of-the-box solution surprised you? Did this solution work?

3. Have you ever experienced a tsunami-like storm that unexpectedly crashed your roof? Did it affect your thinking and believing about God's love for you?

4. Tell about a time when you avoided a cave-in by simply using good sense.

5. How has Isaiah 45:3 worked in your life: "I will give you the treasure of darkness and hidden wealth of secret places"?

2

MONEY CAVE-IN: "WHAT DID YOU PAY FOR THAT?"

In addition to love, there were a number of reasons it made good sense to marry Ken Meberg. To begin with, he was cute, tons of fun, and thought I had good legs. He also thought I was funny, so we both contributed many laughs for each other's enjoyment! But there was another reason marrying Ken made sense to me. He was smart and a business major. I was smart and an English major. Business, money, strategy, and all that stuff put me in a coma. The philosophical and literary implications of Tolstoy put Ken in a coma. We needed each other.

Within a few weeks of our marriage, I began teaching school and Ken began graduate school. Since I was the only one making a salary, even I knew my monthly paycheck of $309 was slim pickings. But being the detail guy he was, Ken sat me down and explained the philosophical and literary implications of our limited income. I understood the apartment rental, cost of utilities, gasoline expense, insurance payments (insurance has got to be the most deadly-boring topic on the planet—I'm convinced hell is full of insurance seminars with required attendance for all residents), church tithing, and food allotment. We agreed to $15 a week for food. Sometimes he bought groceries and sometimes I did: but never, ever did we spend more than $15 a week. There are 323 different recipes for tuna casseroles; I became familiar with them all! In other words, I followed the budget. Oh . . . and I also carpooled to work.

Three years after tuna casseroles, we were in our first home, had a darling baby boy, and Ken was a school principal. We got our first credit card. I understood the basics of how the card worked, but Ken occasionally reminded me of its function and the possibilities of abuse. I always nodded in agreement with what he was saying and quietly wondered why he kept repeating himself.

One morning little Jeff was dazzling me with his first

steps across the living room floor when the doorbell rang. I was surprised to see a young man in a suit, tie, and matching shoes standing there with a warm smile. He asked me if I was by chance a credit card holder, and if he could see the card. That seemed odd to me but my purse was by the door so I pulled out the card. He asked if I would mind handing it to him. Like a moron, I opened the screen door. He reached for it and in a flash pulled huge scissors out of his pocket and cut the card in half. He handed the two pieces back to me, smiled pleasantly, and walked away. I was totally flabbergasted . . . "Wha . . . who . . . why?"

When Ken got home that night I was indignant about the strange man who had come to my door, taken my credit card, and cut it in half. I told Ken we had made a terrible mistake moving to a neighborhood where such criminal acts like that could occur in broad daylight. It was unthinkable!

Ken collapsed in hysterics. I stared at him as he fought to regain his composure, lost it, and collapsed again. Slowly I began to get what had happened that morning. Waiting until Ken stopped hiccupping (he always hiccupped when he laughed hard), I said to him, "You don't mean to tell me you sent that 'suit' to the door to cut my card up, do you?" That set him off again for another ten minutes with equal time for hiccupping. By the way, the "suit guy" was Ken's vice princi-pal. I love that hairbrained solution.

Obviously I had been abusing the card. It was so easy to see a darling little something or other and simply use the card instead of cash. But when I saw a Brown and Jordan patio set on sale and thought the card would be handy for it, too, I'd stretched too far. Ken had to do more than just have a chat with me; we were losing roof shingles and I didn't have sense enough to know it.

One of the leading causes of marital conflict is money issues. Many couples can more easily talk about religion, sex, and politics than they can talk about money. As a result, there's little communication about a subject vastly important for a harmonious relationship. I loved Ken's comedic approach to opening up discussion about the dreaded topic: the budget. It needed to occur. I needed to listen.

Both people in a relationship need to be in agreement about major money matters. At the risk of putting you into one of those comas with which I am so familiar, may I sug-gest some important talk-think points for the maintenance of your roof and the calming of your mate?

I think money secrets are dangerous. If you are in the "I'm going to marry this person" stage, first disclose to each other your salary, debt load, student loans, inheritance, savings, and credit status. Know what the money picture looks like before you marry it. A friend of mine fell head over heels in love with the man who was everything her first husband was not. They did not compare spending patterns, savings preferences, or use of credit. He was smart enough to know she had insurance money from the death of her husband, and I also think he was smart enough to know she was hopelessly smitten with him and would ask no questions.

When they married, she gradually realized he had no savings, was in debt over a failed business, and was paying huge child support payments. His ex-wife kept taking him to court for increased child support. Shingles will soon fly off that roof.

I was watching a talk show during breakfast recently and the host was doing "on the street" interviews with people hurrying to their workplaces. The question posed was, "Do you tell your spouse the price of things you buy, or do you knock off a few dollars to make the purchase seem more reasonable?" One guy said, "I tell her the truth because there would be big trouble if I got caught!" A sweet young woman said, "I always tell him everything!" I hope these people were speaking honestly, because honesty is crucial.

Another crucial money talk point is whether to have joint or separate bank accounts. When Ken and I married, it never occurred to me that we would have separate accounts. We put everything into one pot and drew out from that pot. It made it simpler; each knew what was going on financially.

However now, after being a widow for eighteen years, were I to marry again (perish the thought), I would not think of putting my earnings into a common pot. I have financial systems set up that I want to keep intact. Whatever I have accumulated at my death will go to my children and grandchildren. That is not to say I would oppose a joint account for living expenses (expenses like Brown and Jordan patio furniture).

Another important money issue is being in agreement about large expenditures. I have a friend whose household rule is if it's over $500, let's talk about it. Otherwise, no questions asked. What is important about this is they are in agreement and have set $500 as their limit.

Unfortunately that rule was not an agreement for another friend who is on the brink of bankruptcy and foreclosure on her home. My friend has been a fantastic real estate speculator who made enormous amounts of money buying and selling property. When California real estate was thriving, she bought two homes that were in disrepair. She fixed them up with the intention of "flipping" them and making a profit as she had done in the past. But the real estate market crashed and she is left holding the two investment properties plus her own home, all of which may experience foreclosure. Her husband knew nothing about the debt his wife was incurring until two months ago. He is stunned. She had always taken care of everything and had always done it well. Now they are on the verge of losing all their assets. They should have talked; he should have known; he should have asked. They are on the verge of a huge cave-in.

I believe one of the greatest solutions we can choose for all cave-in prevention is communication. We need to talk to each other, to listen to each other, and to present all the facts as best we know them.

Ken certainly tried to do that with me shortly before he died. Every time he would try to talk to me about "stuff" I would slip into my customary coma. You'd think I would have learned with the careful tutoring I received from him, but obviously I was in the remedial class for thirty years. Three months after his death I began to receive crabby letters from something called a mortgage company. I didn't like their attitude.

Finally I called Luci Swindoll and read her the most recent crabby letter I had received that day. Her response was a mixture of hilarity and disbelief. She said, "Marilyn, do you know the meaning of the word *mortgage*?" I admitted I'd heard the word plenty of times but it had no personal appeal. She said,

"Honey . . . you are going to lose your house if you don't pay your mortgage." I must admit the phrase "lose your house" got my attention. She drove to my home in Laguna Beach and from there drove me to the address of the crabby people.

Apparently the phrase "distraught widow" softened them up a bit. They ultimately became very courteous and even solicitous of my condition. I assured them I would be fine and that I felt sufficiently recovered to never miss another mortgage payment. I paid what I owed, thanked them for their kindness, and Luci and I walked out the door to her car. On our way to lunch I asked her if she would like me to explain the word *mortgage* to her. She died laughing; I paid for lunch.

I narrowly missed a major cave-in simply because of not knowing what I should have known. When Proverbs 22:3 popped into my devotions one morning, I knew beyond a doubt it was high time I became a prudent person! In case you don't remember the verse off-hand, here it is:

A prudent person foresees the danger ahead and takes precautions. The simpleton goes blindly on and suffers the consequences.

My years of being a simpleton had to stop.

The first step was to settle down and think: *What kinds of things must I do to no longer qualify for the presidency of Simpletons Anonymous?* I hired Eclectic Associates, Christian financial planners whom I knew and trusted. I confessed to them I feared I would not be able to "make it" on my own. I had moved directly from my parental home to my married home, and I was scared about managing it successfully.

With their guidance and encouragement, I sold the Laguna Beach home and moved into a wonderful little condominium. The money I made from the Laguna sale paid for the condo; I invested the rest. When I sold the California condo and moved to Texas, I paid cash for the Texas home and again invested the rest. Presently my car is ten years old and paid for. I have one credit card that I pay off at the end of each month; I am debt free. Ken would be proud. I am relieved.

I realize that at my stage in life it was easier to downsize than it may be for you. I no longer have to pay for teeth straightening, soccer shoes, prom dresses, college educations, or a first car. My kids are launched. But whatever your financial burdens may be at this moment, I strongly encourage you to tackle the issue of debt. A credit card feels like a momentary free ride until the bill comes at the end of the month.

When my daughter, Beth, got caught in the vortex of credit card debt two years ago, she contacted a financial planner from her church who has helped her set up a budget. She is slowly paying down her debt and now using one credit card for emergencies only. She has taken charge of her roof maintenance and is relieved to see strong shingles replacing those that were loosening and blowing in the wind.

What's the secret of budget success? Don't buy Brown and Jordan furniture unless you can pay cash! Of course the secret to budget success is cutting down on purchases. Perhaps you need to put a little zip into that boring task and tuck away a small amount each month for fun. Ken and I had what we called our "wild 'n' wooly" sock that collected loose change or even an occasional dollar bill. At the end of the month we'd check to see if there was enough for a pie at Polly's Pie Palace. If not, maybe a hot fudge sundae at Bob's Big Boy. If not, maybe two Bordeaux chocolates at See's Candy. If not, we'd wait until the next month to see if the wild 'n' wooly sock was fatter.

What to think about money boils down to a very simple solution: don't spend what you don't have. Even though large purchases like a car or a house may require a loan, be aware of the monthly payment and make sure it can fit into your budget. If it can't, wait. You may find your present home or apartment can really perk up with a fresh paint job and a few throw pillows. The same principle applies to a car. Keep the engine happy but don't worry about the cracked vinyl seats. Wait for the right time. Your purchases will mean even more to you when you feel they're wisely earned and paid for. You'll also eliminate the noise of loose shingles rattling on your roof.

We've been talking about the value of knowing and thinking as a tool to use in avoiding cave-ins. I simply have to throw the following joke into the mix . . . bear with me. I still think money talk is boring, and jokes help me. See if you can find the thin tie-in to this chapter's subject!

A mother looked out a window and saw Johnny playing church with their three kittens. He had them lined up and was preaching to them. The mother turned around to do some work.

A while later she heard meowing and scratching on the door. She went to the window and saw Johnny baptizing the kittens.

She opened the window and said, "Johnny, stop that! You'll drown those kittens."

Johnny looked at her and said with much conviction in his voice, "They should have thought of that before they joined my church."

In case the tie-in is too elusive, here it is: you must *think*, even if you are a kitten! So OK then, let's talk now about what we believe about money.

The Bible has a lot to say about what we ought to believe

about money. Ecclesiastes 5:10 says, "Those who love money will never have enough. How absurd to think that wealth brings true happiness!" Underscoring this Old Testament teaching about money is the New Testament commentary on this subject found in 1 Timothy 6:10: "For the love of money is at the root of all kinds of evil. And some people, craving money, have wandered from the faith and pierced themselves with many sorrows." Jesus illustrated this teaching by saying, "How hard is it for rich people to enter the Kingdom of God! It is much harder for a rich person to enter the Kingdom of God than for a camel to go through the eye of a needle" (Luke 18:24–25 GNT).

Scripture does not teach that having money is evil; it's the craving, wanting, and seeking after it that can cause soul cave-ins. Balanced thinking about money is expressed in Ecclesiastes 5:19: "And it is a good thing to receive wealth from God and the good health to enjoy it. To enjoy your work and accept your lot in life—that is indeed a gift from God."

My belief about money is to agree with God and know it is He who gives me financial gifts. If I seek after and crave more than He gives to me, I'm flirting with a "root of evil." He is the supplier of all my needs. That does not mean I lie in my hammock waiting for my daily supply. I partner with God and work where He directs me to work. Then, perhaps before dark, I can flop into my hammock and thank God for the "wealth" I'm receiving from Him each day.

Another theme from Scripture about money is giving back to God a portion of what He has given me. The Old Testament law was to give a tenth of everything we have. Deuteronomy 14:23 says, "The purpose of tithing is to teach you always to fear the LORD your God." I interpret that verse to mean tithing reminds me to give back to the Giver and to never stray from the knowledge of where that "gift" originated. If I stray from that truth I am disrespecting God's love and provision for me. I believe in what God clearly teaches about money.

ROOF MAINTENANCE

1. What is your money philosophy? How much does your spouse need to know about your shared income? How do you feel about keeping money secrets?

2. What is your philosophy about credit cards? How do you manage monthly expenses? Are you comfortable with debt?

3. Is there such a thing as "budget success"?

4. How did your parents handle money? Do you have much the same philosophy as they have?

5. What is a good way to teach kids the value of money? Do you think all kids should have an allowance? Instead of an allowance, do you think kids should work for their money?

3

THE ULTIMATE
CAVE-IN: SUICIDE

The film *Harold and Maude* starring Ruth Gordon and Bud Cort is an old classic that dates back to 1971. I have probably seen it seven or eight times. In spite of the morbidity of the subject matter, suicide and death, it is a quirky, funny, and even life-affirming movie that never fails to engage me. Why?

For one thing, I am old and quirky, but I also love great acting and, I must admit, dark humor with a light message. But in spite of my personal oddities, the film deals with a subject I am vitally interested in. Why does anyone choose death over life? I'll give you a brief synopsis of the plotline.

Harold (Bud Cort) is seventeen years old and obsessed with death. He fakes repeated suicide scenes to unsettle his wealthy, self-absorbed mother who endlessly interviews possible girlfriends for Harold, who would rather drive his souped-up hearse around town and attend the funerals of strangers.

At one of those funerals he meets a seventy-nine-year-old woman named Maude (Ruth Gordon) who also attends funerals of strangers but not because she is obsessed with death; she is obsessed with life. For her, death is a beautiful transition from one state of being to a better state of being. She revels in every funeral she attends. Harold falls in love with this free-spirited and eccentric woman. Their relationship contributes to Harold's learning how to embrace life.

In one of the early scenes, Harold takes Maude on a picnic to his favorite spot: a wrecking yard. When he asks her if she likes the spot, she says it has a certain charm but then asks Harold if "the wrecking yard is enough."

Ultimately, Harold wants more than a wrecking yard. He comes to realize his melodramatic suicide stagings are pointless; his spirit is already dead. Maude gives him the inspiration to see life's beauty and fun—available to anyone who has the eyes to see it and the will to choose it.

So, is the decision to live about no longer see your life as a wrecking yard? Is it just a matter of willing yourself into seeing life's beauty and fun, getting a grip and moving on as Harold did? For many, the motivation to choose life is far more complicated than that.

For those who commit suicide, there is an anguish of soul so profoundly overwhelming there is no available energy left that enables them to make a life-affirming choice. That kind of anguish accounts for the sobering statistic from U.S. Centers for Disease Control, stating suicides outnumber homicides and take the lives of twice as many people as HIV/AIDS. In young people between the ages of fifteen and twenty it ranks as the third leading cause of death. These statistics are about an inability to choose life. We need to consider these statistics with compassion and increased understanding. Because behind these numbers are individuals whose anguish became too great to bear.

I received a letter from a grieving grandmother who could not understand why her grandson (age sixteen) drove his car into the parking lot of his church and shot himself. She wrote, "He was a good kid; very well liked. His father died in an explosion when my grandson was just a baby. My daughter raised him alone until just recently when she remarried. Everyone says she had done a remarkable job as a single mom. The people in this small community are in shock. No one can figure out why he would do such a thing."

There's a reason why this boy chose death over life. For him, the wrecking yard of his life was no longer manageable. The question of what was going on in his soul prior to pulling the trigger is excruciating. What kind of inner anguish was he experiencing prior to deciding to get a gun, driving to the church, and then doing the unthinkable? We know it was not an impulse; apparently it was a decision. Again the question, why? There are a few clues we could speculate about but of course they are only speculations. Nevertheless, there are some "tracers" that can take us back to a point of origin for this boy's pain. Let's track some of those tracers.

To begin with, we want to pay close attention to any behavior that suggests suicidal inclinations: mood changes, depression, hopelessness, low self-esteem, overwhelming life challenges, and severe health problems. In the case of this grandson, I am struck by a couple of tracer facts. His father died when the boy was a baby. One might think that would not be a major loss because he never knew his father. In spite of the boy's age when he lost his dad, he never had the "Daddy need" satisfied. That loss, though unidentified, creates a hole in the soul that never fills in. We assume Mom did the best she could to make up for her son's loss, but she still could never be Daddy. That's a hard reality.

With mother's recent remarriage there is yet another dynamic for this young man to deal with. Did the remarriage feel like another loss—the loss of his mother? How did the stepfather treat him? Did the boy struggle with feeling he did not belong anywhere or to anyone? Did he feel he'd lost all human anchoring?

I want to sidetrack here for a minute and throw out a few thoughts about remarriage. These realities may have impacted this young man. I'm deeply concerned about the emotional effect of remarriage on children. It is only natural that lonely moms or dads long for a new life and an opportunity to experience a healthy marriage. One of the compelling arguments for remarriage is the desire parents have for the kids to see how a good relationship works. Parents want to model the harmony and love it is possible to have in a healthy marriage environment, which may be a direct contrast to the previous marriage. That is a commendable goal, but all too often old baggage is carried into the new marriage. The goal then may not be realized. To avoid that, or at least eliminate some of those boxes of baggage, I strongly suggest making marriage counseling a priority. If there is no counseling, resulting in new behavior, the kids may see a replay of what they just left. That is devastating to their internal balance and security.

But even if the old baggage is kept to a minivan, the kids from each "side" have to somehow learn to accommodate each other. They may not have chosen to share bathrooms, beds, toys, food, or daily patterns. And they surely did not intend to share their parent. That is a huge adjustment for kids and many don't make that adjustment well. We frequently hear people say, "Kids are resilient—they can take a lot." Kids may survive but they don't necessarily thrive.

I think we owe the kids God gifted us with our full parental attention and total commitment. That may mean we would be wise to postpone our own needs for a period of time. That does not mean we are selfless to the point of having no life separate from our children. But I do think the stability we can offer our children is more important than a new mate with his/her kids.

Kids need to know they are a priority. They need to see you at their soccer games, bassoon recitals (mercy!), choir concerts, Christmas pageants, and as many other activities as your schedule can accommodate. Your presence communicates to them that they matter. They assume then there is value in who they are and what they do.

Perhaps even more important, they need to know your

ear is available to them. You communicate by your availability that you want to hear whatever they want to say. They will not always have such need of your focused attention but for the time they are in need of you, it's good to be there.

You may be muttering to yourself words like, "Good grief, Marilyn . . . are you blaming that boy's suicide on the fact he never had a father and his mother remarried?" There are undoubtedly many unknowns that caused that boy to think, *Life is too hard, and I'm not up for it.* He may have been battling depression for years. Perhaps he was in a drug-alcohol cycle from which he couldn't break free. Whatever all the other unknowns may have been, they convinced him to say no to life. Surely there are things we can learn from this kind of tragedy. So then let's turn our attention to what we think about suicide and how we can know more about it.

There are a number of "faulty thinkings" about suicide, suicide myths. Remembering that a myth is fiction or, at best, a half truth, we should know then what those myths are. Here are three of the most common:

MYTH 1: A person is more likely to commit suicide if it has first been discussed, so stay away from that kind of talking.

FACT: Studies show that is not the case. If someone kills herself/himself it is because a decision has been made to do so. Talking about it does not increase the commitment to do it.

MYTH 2: Suicide is an irrational and impulsive act.

FACT: Studies indicate the decision was first thought about and planned for. Rarely is a suicide "out of the blue." A therapist who suspects a suicidal inclination always checks for a plan.

MYTH 3: Suicidal attempts that failed were never really serious in the first place.

FACT: Research indicates a great percentage of those who committed suicide made previous attempts or threats. As the number of attempts increases so does the likelihood that a future attempt will be fatal.

In looking at some of the suicide myths, which reflect faulty thinking, there are three basic known truths about people who commit suicide. These truths are also helpful for us to know. They are:

1. Most suicidal people do not want to end their biological existence. Instead, they want to end their psychological pain and suffering.

2. Most suicidal people tell someone that they are thinking about suicide as a means of coping with their pain.

3. Most suicidal people have psychological problems, social problems, and poor methods for coping with pain.

Another faulty thought, which is anguishing to those who loved the person, is *Maybe I could have prevented it.* I have some dear friends whose mother took her life several months ago. Apparently mother had been threatening to kill herself for fifty years. My friends cannot remember a time as they were growing up that the fear of mom "ending it" did not hover over their daily living.

Life with their mother had always been an emotional roller-coaster, but when she actually did what she'd threatened to do for so many years, the family was stunned. Then the heart-rending question for them all became, "Did we do enough for her? Could we have prevented this in some way?" Self-accusing thoughts like, *Surely someone, somehow, and at some time could have said or done just the right thing and saved her from herself . . . surely . . .*

It is helpful to know one of the most reliable predictors of suicide is the diagnosis of Major Depressive Disorder. Simply stated, that means depression has moved from the category of a characteristic to a disorder. The emotions, the mind, and the behavior become disordered, which can throw life into a chaotic state. In addition to major depression, a diagnosis of schizophrenia, bipolar disorder, or sever borderline personality disorder is also a major influence for suicide. I am convinced my friends' mother suffered from one or several of those mental disorders. If that is the case, her family can be encouraged to realize they may have tried as hard as they possibly could but still not have prevented her decision.

Let's explore another facet of what we think about suicide with this question: is there ever a time when taking one's life is a justifiable and wise decision?

A man I know was recently diagnosed with Huntington's disease. According to the *Columbia Encyclopedia,* this disease is hereditary. Fifty percent of the offspring of an affected parent inherit the gene that inevitably leads to Huntington's. It is an acute disturbance of the central nervous system usually beginning in middle age. It is characterized by involuntary muscular movements and progressive intellectual deterioration. The psychiatric disturbances range from personality changes, involving apathy and irritability, to bipolar or schizophrenic illness. At this time, there is no way to stop or reverse the course of Huntington's.

Needless to say, this man is devastated. So is his wife and so are their three teenagers. He knew nothing of his biological history, only that he'd been adopted by a loving missionary couple who fell in love with him as a little five-year-old boy living in a Romanian orphanage.

He is now educating himself on his disease and realizing there is no hope of a cure. His desire is to spare his wife and children from witnessing the awful progression and hopelessness of his illness. He wants to take his life. His scriptural justification is John 15:13: "The greatest love is shown when people lay down their lives for their friends." He believes he would be doing his family a loving favor.

There is nothing in me that judges this man for what he wants to do. While he can still think, he wants to make a considered choice about what his family will have to endure if he lives. Wanting to spare them, as well as himself, the desire to end his life is perfectly logical. The question is, is it spiritually admissible? The answer is no. Much as human logic may make a defense for the taking of life, there is no biblical permission.

"Wait a minute," you say. "What about capital punishment, self-defense, or war? Some issues are gray, Marilyn, you cannot dogmatically state there's no biblical permission for the taking of life!"

Scripture teaches there is a sanctity about all life and that sanctity is to be respected. Paul makes that teaching clear when he talks about our bodies and that they are to be reverenced because they are the temples in which the spirit of God lives (1 Corinthians 3:16–17). He also states in 1 Corinthians 6:13, 15: "Our bodies . . . were made for the Lord, and the Lord cares about our bodies. . . . Don't you realize that your bodies are actually parts of Christ?"

Much as I yearn to say it is biblically permissible to take our lives to avoid a horrible death, I have to recognize my body is spiritually connected to the body of Christ. I cannot destroy what is not mine to destroy.

This discussion leads us to even more specific consideration concerning the spiritual consequences of suicide. Many believe those who take their lives will not go to heaven. Fear of hell has kept many persons tethered to this earth. Scripture leads me to believe a Christian who commits suicide does not get the "death penalty" of hell. When Jesus died on the cross for the sins of the world, all sin was taken to the cross. Jesus took on Himself the death penalty for our sin. He died for it all; that would include suicide.

My responsibility is to receive His gift of forgiveness for the sin Jesus died for. I do that by confessing my sin to Him and receiving His cleansing. That forgiveness sets me free from what would have condemned me. Isaiah 44:22 says, "I have swept away your sins like the morning mists. I have scattered your offenses like the clouds. Oh, return to me, for I have paid the price to set you free."

There are those who believe that since suicide is a premeditated murder, the suicide victim cannot go to heaven because the sin was not confessed. That thinking troubles me because it implies if we have a sin of any kind, even in our thinking, we would be condemned by it in the event of our sudden death. In other words, we would need to be continually "confessed up" or that unconfessed sin would doom us to eternal punishment. That is living under constant condemnation.

For example, if I am thinking uncharitable thoughts about the driver in front of me and am suddenly hit head-on by an eighteen-wheeler, which causes my death, do I go to hell because of my thoughts prior to my death? Does that make sense? We are invited to live in the amazing grace of Romans 8:1–2. Let's read this verse from *The Message* translation:

With the arrival of Jesus, the Messiah, that fateful dilemma is resolved. Those who enter into Christ's being-here-for-us no longer have to live under a continuous, low-lying black cloud. A new power is in operation. The Spirit of life in Christ, like a strong wind, has magnificently cleared the air, freeing you from a fated lifetime of brutal tyranny at the hands of sin and death.

A lifetime of "brutal tyranny" is one in which I live in constant dread of an eighteen-wheeler suddenly descending upon me at a moment of sinful thinking.

Admittedly, we do not have definitive or specific answers for the question: what is the eternal destination for one who takes his/her life? But we do have specific and definitive promises from God. Read these nurturing words:

> His huge outstretched arms protect you—under them you're perfectly safe; his arms fend off all harm.
>
> (Psalm 91:4 MSG)

> I will never desert you nor will I ever forsake you.
>
> (Hebrews 13:5 NASB)

> The LORD is near to the brokenhearted.
>
> (Psalm 34:18 NASB)

> I am holding you by your right hand.
>
> (Isaiah 41:13)

I will not abandon you.

(John 14:18)

Do not these amazing promises apply to all of us all the time? Does it make sense those promises apply only to those who are not suicidal? Do not these promises wrap themselves around any anguished heart that has lost hope?

God did not will the sixteen-year-old boy's suicide, the mother's suicide, or the man with Huntington's who is contemplating it. But not one of them, or any of us, is alone in our anguish. Psalm 31:7 says that God cares about the anguish of my soul. Scripture teaches us this and we can believe God's caring heart is fully engaged with ours and He will never, ever leave us alone.

ROOF MAINTENANCE

1. Have you known anyone who has committed suicide?

2. Do you think the person who commits suicide loses her or his faith in God? Do you think heaven is only for those who choose to stay on this earth?

3. Is there anything in you that feels judgmental about the person who chooses to take her or his life?

4. What can you say to family members who have lost someone to suicide?

5. Do you think a person who knows Christ as Savior but takes his or her life can be sure of going to heaven?

RESOURCES FOR FURTHER STUDY:

1. The National Strategy for Suicide Prevention (http://mentalhealth.samhsa.gov/SuicidePrevention/) provides a wide variety of articles and statistics on suicide, specifically regarding youth, the elderly, suicide methods, and mental illness.

2. The National Youth Violence Prevention Resource Center (www.safeyouth.org) is a federal resource for professionals, parents, and youth working to prevent violence committed by and against young people.

3. See Suicide Awareness Voices of Education (www.save.org) for information about depression and suicide as well as suicide prevention information.

4

INFIDELITY CAVE-IN

A lady walked into a drugstore and told the pharmacist she wanted some cyanide. The pharmacist said, "Why in the world do you need cyanide?" The lady then explained she needed it to poison her husband. The pharmacist's eyes grew enormous, and then he said, "Lord have mercy! I can't give you cyanide to kill your husband; that's against the law. I'll lose my license. Not only that, we both will be thrown in jail. No, absolutely not. I can't sell you any cyanide!" The woman reached into her purse and pulled out a picture of her husband in bed with the pharmacist's wife. He looked at the picture and then slowly replied, "Well now . . . you didn't tell me you had a prescription."

Recently there has been relentless media coverage of a very public cave-in. A prominent politician has just confessed to an affair. It had been hidden for a year by lies and denials of what now has become an obvious reality.

"No, that is not my baby! Yes, I showed very poor judgment. I confessed it to my wife. . . . She has forgiven me. . . . But no, that is not my baby."

As of this writing, it appears the man's messy cave-in is burying future political aspirations, the trust of a nation that judges the betrayal of his terminally ill wife, and empathy for the looks of confusion on the faces of his young children. What happens when he becomes the sole parent after they lose their mother? Will he be a nurturing harbor for their pain? How will they survive the shock waves of their father's infidelity? Is there a "love child"? What then?

In addition to those questions we wonder, "What were you thinking? How will you ever crawl out from beneath the cave-in you initiated?" These are all crucial questions and ones that call for an answer. And there are many who are asking themselves these very same questions.

As I've said, there's always a solution for every cave-in, and incidentally, that solution is not cyanide. However, I did hear one hairbrained solution for universal cave-ins, proposed by Sir Dingle Mackintosh Foot, a British elder statesman. He said that problems stemming from poor judgment can be cured with good nutrition: "If the Americans had a substantial breakfast of bacon and eggs, they wouldn't have problems like Watergate. A proper breakfast adds to your judgments. You can't expect to start the day on cereals, shredded wheat and muck like that."

Though fortifying, a diet of bacon and eggs will not keep the roof sturdy, nor will it repair the roof once it caves in. The repair work requires a conscientious rethink and a genuine recommitment to a discarded value system.

Infidelity occurs for one of two reasons: lust or love. For Old Testament king David, it was lust. You'll remember he was napping late in the afternoon on the rooftop of his palace. It was a typically hot afternoon there in Israel. David was seeking a breeze to refresh him. Instead, he saw the beautiful Bathsheba bathing on her rooftop. He was more than refreshed. Second Samuel 11:4 says, "David sent for her; and when she came to the palace, he slept with her." That poor judgment can hardly be blamed on shredded wheat.

Their sleepover produced a pregnancy. The consequences of David's sin began almost immediately. Instead of insisting, "That is not my baby," he devised a plan to bring Bathsheba's husband home from war, hoping that they would immediately sleep together, and then her pregnancy would appear to be the result of their marital union. But Uriah, the husband, did not want to leave the soldiers under his command. He asked David, "How could I go home to wine and dine and sleep with my wife? I swear that I will never be guilty of acting like that" (2 Sam. 11:11). Uriah was a sensitive and caring military leader; the well-being of his men came before his own.

David, feeling trapped by the moral cave-in of his own choice, decides on a drastic solution. Uriah must be positioned in such a way that he dies in battle. David would then marry the pregnant widow Bathsheba. The plan is put in place: Uriah is killed; Bathsheba marries King David. It was a perfect cave-in solution: no witnesses.

But we, as believers in an all-knowing and all-seeing God, understand that there is always at least one witness to our sin—God. He hates sin. He had a few words to say to David through his prophet Nathan:

The LORD, the God of Israel, says, "I anointed you King of Israel and saved you from the power of Saul. . . . Why, then, have you despised the word of the LORD and done this horrible deed? For you have murdered Uriah and stolen his wife. . . . Because of what you have done, I, the LORD, will cause your own household to rebel against you. I will give your wives to another man, and he will go to bed with them in public view. You did it secretly, but I will do this to you openly in the sight of all Israel."

(2 Sam. 12:7, 9–11)

In addition to these consequences of David's sin, God told David his child, soon to be born, would die; he did. The question God posed to David was, "Why . . . after all I did for you?" Guilt. David was buried in it.

The guilt from infidelity burns like an inextinguishable ember deeply embedded in the lining of the soul. That coal burns brightly, whether the infidelity is discovered or not. Because of that, there is often a sense of relief when the moment of truth arrives. At long last the secret is out. The tension of maintaining a double life that demands managing logistics, erasing e-mails, hiding cell phones, camouflaging expenses, and hiding meeting places is exhausting. So why do we do it? Let's talk about a few "whys."

In spite of knowing better, many people buy into Satan's favorite lie: there's more. The lie says, "There's more excitement, greater intimacy, and deeper love out there; you can have more." Because the enemy of our soul is a crafty jerk, he knows full well that lie is hard to resist. It worked on Eve; it works on us. Who doesn't want *more*?

Back in the days when I was teaching in the public school

system, a fellow teacher ten years older than I began to confide in me about her various marital indiscretions. Because we frequently shared an assigned playground duty, I couldn't always escape her. Hearing about her X-rated escapades provided a stark contrast to watching children playing kickball.

I finally asked her one morning why she was such a party girl. Her response was, "When you've been married a few more years, Marilyn, you'll want more. I just need more than my husband can give me. You'll learn that soon enough." I asked if her husband knew how she felt and what would happen if she got caught. Her response was, "He travels a lot—he probably does what I do. Besides, the risk of getting caught makes it more fun." That woman was out of control—her shingles were getting looser by the day. Also, that woman wasn't wanting more love; her drive was fueled by lust. I now realize her need for more and more sexual pleasure stemmed from addiction (more about sexual addiction in chapter 8).

So what about Christians? Why do they, too, get caught in the net of Satan's lie, "There's more"? Shouldn't we know better? What happens to us that causes vulnerability to the point of infidelity?

One of Satan's most successful ploys with us Christians is to offer the "more" lie in the form of friendships. What is more innocent and valuable, safe and soul building than friendship? But there are some we need to be careful about.

I have come to the conclusion that male-female friendships are, more often than not, dangerous. I know this sounds crabby, but I don't recommend them. Here's why: No matter how carefully it may be monitored, there is no escaping male-female underlying sexual tension. Of course some men have greater appeal than others just as some women are more appealing than others. But all have enormous appeal once they touch the soul of someone who has not previously felt appreciated, attractive, gifted, clever, charming, entertaining, competent, wise . . . the list goes on.

The person who provides those missing pieces on the "want more" list gets heart attention. The lie of "there's more" no longer appears to be a lie. The "more" is right there in the office, the church planning committee, the divorce recovery group, the worship team, PTA, soccer team . . . and that's just the short list.

As each of the "more" persons begins to share increasingly about his or her life, a level of confidentiality is established. That confidentiality builds to a plateau where the emotions become engaged. That buildup of mutual emotion can lead to romantic attachment. That romantic attachment can lead to . . . and there you have it.

So what does one do? Run from all people for fear you may talk to, care about, or share with? I think there are some sensible questions we can ask ourselves in an effort to continually monitor male/female relatedness. I don't recommend running; I do recommend thinking. And after thinking, be aware.

The following cautions for men and women are just common sense, but they may highlight the need for you to nudge away from a potentially unsafe "more" person. Incidentally, the "more" person is not unsafe; emotions are. Ask yourself:

1. Do you consider your "more person" a soul mate?

2. Does your "more person" know more about you than your spouse knows?

3. Have you confided private and personal weaknesses in your marriage?

4. Would you be uncomfortable if your spouse knew all you had confided?

5. Would you feel uncomfortable if your spouse joined in on all future times of being with your "more person"?

6. Do you and your "more person" flirt with each other?

7. Have you imaged what it would be like to have sex with your "more person"?

8. Have you mutually agreed each of you feels sexual chemistry?

If the answer is yes to the last three questions, your roof shingles are shaking. I suggest you run; then get out your repair kit. Since a part of our repair kit is to think, let's do some thinking on the origins of infidelity.

As I said earlier, infidelity is fueled by lust (King David) or love (your "more person"). But both categories are morally challenged. Even if you haven't acted upon your sexual attraction to the "more person," if you've thought about it, there's a potential cave-in. Sin takes place first in the mind. What are you thinking? Know those thoughts and where they are leading you. Guard your mind. We have no evidence King David stopped to examine his thoughts. Apparently the only thinking he did was to strategize how long it would take to get Bathsheba out of her house and into his. Lust has limited brain power; it travels too quickly.

Let's loop back and take a second look at how the enemy of our soul operates. His sole intent is to watch the moral and physical destruction of God's people. A method that has worked for him from the beginning of time is to bait a hook and dangle it in front of each of us. What's the bait? *More.* Whenever our eagerness for more causes us to swallow the bait, we're hooked. Our enemy jeers, salivates, and cheers every time. He chalks up another victory on his scoreboard; then he rebaits.

Let's take a look now at how you believe. Maybe the following questions can clarify your beliefs.

After infidelity, do you believe . . .

1. you have a moral obligation to stay in your marriage?

2. you must stay for the sake of the children?

3. it's God's will for you to stay?

4. God will not bless your life if you leave?

5. the children will blame you for the marriage failure if you leave?

6. you have somehow failed your spouse so it's actually your fault?

7. you have a spiritual obligation to forgive?

8. your spouse does not deserve forgiveness?

9. you will never trust again?

10. this marriage was never God's will in the first place?

Few cave-ins are more difficult to survive than those caused by infidelity. Knowing that the lie of "more" fuels infidelity does little to rebuild the splintered remains littering the cave floor. Roughly 35 percent of those marriages survive the betrayal of infidelity. You may believe your marriage will be one of the 35 percent. On the other hand, you may believe there's no way it will survive and you have no intention of even attempting to repair that marital roof.

No matter which choice you make, to stay or leave, I strongly advise you to have Christian professional counsel. Your wounds are so deep, you need someone to walk you through the steps leading to your healing. One of the best first steps I know is an intensive weekend at a New Life Ministries Clinic (newlife.com or 1-800-639-5433). God uses human beings to accomplish His divine goal; that goal is healing for you. Don't remain buried beneath the rubble of your cave-in. God promises to bring good from all things, even this.

I want to say a final word about a "more person." One of the ways God can bring good from a cave-in as disastrous as infidelity is for us to come to the realization that He, the God of all creation, is the ultimate "more person."

He knows all our insecurities, weaknesses, vulnerabilities, longings, secrets, shame, guilt, and deep cravings to be loved. He does not ask us to be someone we are not. We don't have to wear makeup, smell good, have perfect hair, polished nails or stylish clothes. We can wear heels or go barefoot; we can be sophisticated or corny. We can't shock Him. We can be totally human and not fear rejection because of it. He has one desire—that we choose Him to be our ultimate "more person."

ROOF MAINTENANCE

1. Do you agree or disagree with this statement: "male-female friendships are, more often than not. dangerous"?

2. Do you think there is such a thing as "innocent flirting"? What motivates a person to flirt?

3. Do you feel you have a moral obligation to stay in your marriage in spite of infidelity?

4. What do you think are ways to rebuild trust with a spouse who has betrayed you?

5. Is it ever appropriate for your kids to know their dad cheated on you? Should you lie to cover up for him?

5

TOO HEAVY FOR THE ROOF: SURELY NOT MY FAMILY MEMBERS

During my neurosis-producing two years of living on "Lonely Acres" (forty acres of remote property purchased for the purpose of providing a healing respite for my burned-out pastor father), I developed a number of solutions for personal loneliness as well as fear. Because I am a social creature who thrives on people, Lonely Acres was not a healing respite for me.

We lived in a darling little house my father built (he was extremely "handy") surrounded by evergreen trees. Rarely was there a sound other than that produced by nature. One of the nature sounds I consistently found unsettling was the nighttime howling of coyotes. I was sure there were billions of them and that they were stealthily creeping toward my bedroom destined to arrive anytime after eight o'clock p.m., my bedtime. I formulated a solution meant to calm my fears. This solution could come under the category of hairbrained, but it worked for me.

Each night after the usual bedtime nurturance of a story, prayer, and placement of my bucket (a different neurotic ritual), my mother would leave the room and turn off the light. After assessing the possible distance between the coyotes and myself, I began to tell myself jokes. There were five or six jokes that never failed to make me laugh. My parents, who were in the living room which was probably only twenty feet away, would hear the periodic sounds of chuckling followed by muffled sounds as I told myself the next joke. The highlight experience for them was when they heard the hearty out-loud laugh that signaled I'd told the best joke I always save for last. Dad would say, "That must have been the flagpole joke." Or mother might say, "No, that was a bigger laugh, I think it was the fish joke." They knew those were the two best final jokes. I'd choose to tell one and save the other for the next night. Of course, if the coyotes were peering in the window, I'd tell both jokes.

One morning, in reference to my bedtime joke ritual, my Dad said, "You know, Marilyn, you are just a few bubbles off plumb; I love that about you. It proves you are a true Ricker . . . all Rickers are a few bubbles off plumb." I knew my father's "off-plumb" ways delighted my mother, so I felt pleased to spring from such a rich heritage.

Several weeks ago I read in the newspaper of a solution to a problem that so appealed to my "off-plumb" inclination I laughed out loud. I've repeated it to a few people since reading it; the general response is, "What?" That verbal response, followed by a head-cock, tells me I may stand alone in my appreciation of this solution. See what you think.

As of this writing, officials in St. Paul, Minnesota plan to mix a contraceptive, OvoControl P, with birdseed to reduce the local pigeon population and clean up the streets. They are motivated to take this action because the Republican National Convention is coming to town. The city will put the plan into action immediately by mixing the contraceptive and birdseed in the feeders on top of their city buildings. Any reader who is concerned about the humane treatment of the pigeons was assured the plan had the approval of People for the Ethical Treatment of Animals.

After reading this piece, I wondered if anyone had considered the future confusion of the pigeons as they tried to figure why there were fewer baby pigeons around the Christmas tree in December.

What I love about this account is the people in St. Paul realized they had a problem that needed a solution. It was an out-of-the-box solution but there is no reason to believe it will not be effective. Time will tell.

This anecdote has a broader message for us than simply pigeon control in St. Paul. That message can be applied to any of us attempting to live with a challenging situation we need to change. What's the message? First, there's always a solution. Second, we may have overlooked it because it's so simple.

The challenge we'll look at in this chapter has to do with emotional endurance. The roof becomes a metaphor for how much weight we can bear up under until we have an emotional cave-in. What's weighing us down? People who have flown in, settled on our roof, and, like the pigeons, haven't a clue they have become a burden.

Who are these people? All too often they are family members. This realization makes most of us feel guilty. After all, family members are supposed to love each other, accept, support, and be loyal to each other. They aren't supposed to compete, gossip, or fight. Thanksgiving, Christmas, birthdays, and family celebrations are supposed to be harmonious. We think the words "Let's just try to get along" should not precede those events.

Since what I have described is so familiar to most of us, it makes for great television entertainment. We laugh and feel as if we aren't alone as we watch the sometimes insensitive and inappropriate behavior of someone else's family members being dramatized.

One of my all-time favorite television shows is *Everybody Loves Raymond*. The behavior of Raymond's father, Frank, is beyond insensitive and inappropriate. His favorite things in life are food and the TV remote. Raymond's mother, Marie, is equally inappropriate and insensitive but more subtle. When Debra, Raymond's wife, wants to start her own tradition by hosting a Thanksgiving fish dinner for both families, Marie insists on bringing a turkey for those who love American history.

Raymond's parents live next door. They walk in without knocking, enter into each social event without invitation, and are hurt if not consulted about all family matters. Raymond does not discourage their behavior because he, too, continually pops in and out of their house and finds himself drawn into the domestic dramas of his parents. Also, if the truth were known, Raymond prefers his mother's cooking to Debra's so he frequently snacks there.

One wonders if Debra feels the weight of these people who appear as clueless as pigeons. Or, is she just as clueless as those on the roof? Does she know it's inappropriate for Marie to compete against her for Raymond's love? Does she know Frank should not be allowed to walk in the house, grab the TV remote, and yell out, "Got any snacks?" Is Raymond aware he needs to grow up? Are any of them aware of a sanity-saver called "boundaries"?

A sanity-saver boundary can be the simple word no. "No, you cannot pop in and out of my house without an invitation. No, you cannot take the TV remote and yell for snacks. No, you will not decide what I am serving for Thanksgiving dinner. And no, unless we ask, do not make our business your business." A clearly stated, acted-upon "no" will generally cause roof-sitters to take flight. When they do, you'll have more room up there and less sag. What a simple solution. But many of us don't think to use the word—it's not in our vocabulary.

Establishing a boundary is obvious to us when it deals with physical or geographical matters. I know where my property ends and my neighbor's begins. Where it could become confusing is if there is no fence. "Do our properties run together? Did I plant pansies on your side when I thought I was on my side?" A fence serves as a boundary. You end where I begin. And if you want flowers from my side, I would prefer you ask rather than take what you feel like when you feel like it. That is not being cranky; it is establishing a boundary. A typical roof-sitter would swoop down and take flowers no matter which side they are on. They don't "get" boundaries.

A boundary enables us to maintain emotional endurance and provides a strong roof. The key to emotional endurance is knowing where I begin and you end. When that is threatened, the word *no* is needed. But what if you don't understand where you begin and where you end? What if you not only don't know your beginning or end, but don't know you have a right to a beginning and an end? What if you think whatever I have and whoever I am is up for grabs? That you should take what you want or need anytime?

God immediately set a boundary for Adam and Eve when He placed them in Eden. Every beautiful and delicious fruit was up for grabs. Whatever they wanted and whenever they wanted it was OK with God; everything, that is, except the fruit of one tree. That tree was a "no" tree. Don't touch it; don't eat it. Plain, simple boundary.

Scripture teaches that our worth and value are not to be

touched. They are not up for grabs. There is a "NO" placed upon the souls of His beloved creation, which in essence says, "Don't you dare defile My cherished treasure, the work of My hands, the temple in which I live, the life for whom I died."

Our beginning began the moment we were conceived. Psalm 139:16 reads: "Like an open book, you watched me grow from conception to birth; all the stages of my life were spread out before you, the days of my life all prepared before I'd even lived one day" (MSG). Where we begin is in the mind of God. We will conclude in the arms of God. In the meantime, there is a "no" meant to protect us from any behavior that says we are not God's beloved. We live by divine intent, a God-given right to claim. Therefore, there are times we must say no.

Knowing and believing we have the right to the "no" boundary, let's loop back to Raymond's mother, Marie. Her idea of being a mother was to continue doing what a loving mother does: feed when hungry, give Band-Aids when bleeding, comfort when hurting, advise when confused, wash dirty clothes, iron wrinkled pants, carpool to school, make cupcakes for the fourth grade Valentine party, and meet needs anytime, anyplace. And this, as mothers know, is the short list of "mother doings."

All those "doings" were appropriate when Raymond was a

child and living with his parents. But when he married, he was to leave home and establish a new home: his and that of his wife and children. A part of establishing a new home is creating a new boundary. That new boundary was for Marie to recognize she no longer did the mother "doings." It was no longer appropriate for her to cook, clean, and be the mother-caretaker. Raymond's stated boundary should have been: "Mom, Debra cooks my meals now. You don't pop over with daily casseroles, or gather up my laundry, clean the bathroom, or dust the furniture."

Marie did not understand that a boundary that says no does not mean love no longer exists. It means the household is under new management. Love exists, but appropriate boundaries have been created. Love accepts and lives by those new boundaries.

Like Marie, many mothers just don't get it. The daughter marries, has a new life with appropriate and new allegiances, and Mother feels "bruised." She is no longer consulted as she once was and, mercy, this is the worst, daughter no longer has as much time to devote to mother. If mother continues to sit on the roof, the roof will get heavier and heavier under the weight of mother's hurt feelings.

Back in my counseling days, I worked with a mother and daughter who were struggling in their relationship.

The recently married daughter did not realize she had a right to a "no" boundary. It felt too cold and ungrateful to say no to her mother's many demands for time and attention. To make matters worse, Mother did "that thing," which was to make herself indispensable to the daughter. That continued the sense of dependency on mother. Here's how it worked: Mother would suggest a shopping day, which meant many lovely new clothes for daughter. She then felt guilty about the money spent for those clothes and felt she needed to "repay" mother by carving out time she did not have. This also created problems in the marriage because mother paid for what husband could not afford. He felt "less than" but obligated as well because father-in-law gave him a large sum of money for a new business. All these seemingly generous gestures came with a hook: dependence. "We know you cannot manage without us." That was felt, not stated.

The backlash of adult dependence is resentment. That is followed by guilt. "I resent my dependence on you, but I feel guilty about that because of all you do for me." Emotional endurance is running out and the roof is really sagging now. What's the solution?

The solution is the short, simple "no" boundary. "Mom, Dad, we appreciate so much your generosity to us. But we are realizing that generosity causes us to depend on you instead of each other. It is not good for us to continue to live like kids who need Mom and Dad to keep our financial boat afloat. We need to learn the discipline of living with less and the dignity of floating that boat through our own efforts and judgment."

The goal of the counseling sessions I was having with this mother and daughter was to encourage the daughter to realize she was entitled to use the "no" boundary with her mother. It was sound psychology to separate from the mother's insistence that she have as much access to her daughter as she had always had. And it was scriptural. Genesis 2:24 explains that a man should leaves his father and mother and be joined to his wife. Mother insisted she was not refusing to accept that biblical principle, she was merely extending gestures of love to her daughter. "After all," she said, "loving is another biblical principle!"

This was a tough one because of course loving is a scriptural principle. A "no" boundary does not lack love, it defines "where I begin and where you end." Mother was so fused with her daughter, the only recourse the daughter had was to use the profound but simple no with her mother. The result was that mother flew off the heavily sagging roof but she felt bruised, misunderstood, and rejected. Only time will tell if the "no " solution will ever make sense to mother and not sound unloving.

The same "no" boundary is wise for anyone who feels the need to establish independence. For those who truly want to leave home, I suggest relocating for a year. Learn to manage your own finances, relationships, spiritual life, habits, and patterns. The best way to learn what you're made of is to test it in an environment without a safety net clutched by anxious parents. It is impossible to have healthy connectedness without knowing healthy separateness. Each of us needs to learn our own value, competence, and strength, which comes when we depend on the individual gifts God has placed within us. And not only has He placed within us gifts, He places within us His Spirit. We would all benefit from the example of Jesus who separated Himself from everyone to fast and pray for forty days. In doing so, Jesus connected more deeply with the Holy Spirit within Him, which prepared Him for His earthy ministry.

The hardest-to-deal-with family member who sags the roof and drains endurance is the one who hurts you deeply and won't admit it. That may be a parent who can't be pleased, a sister who convincingly spreads rumors and lies about you, or a brother who delights in saying you've always been unattractive, clumsy, and dumb. It could be a grandmother who questions the sincerity of your Christian faith because you drink wine.

Crystal was a young woman I counseled whose roof-sitter was an older brother who refused to admit or take responsibility for her sexual abuse as a child. She was ten years old when it started. He would come into her room at night, fondle her, and insist she fondle him. He was four years older, and at first she thought he would stop this nightly ritual. Instead, it continued, and when she was thirteen he began to penetrate her regularly. He told her he did these things because she was special and they were acts of love. He was never rough or mean; just persistent. What was most devastating to her was she had come to enjoy it. That guilt alone threatened to cave the roof in.

Crystal received a lot of good counseling before I met her. Her abuse produced an eating disorder as well as depression. When we began to work together she just wanted her brother to say he was sorry and ask for forgiveness. When confronted, he told Crystal there was nothing to apologize for, because what she claimed happened did not happen at all. He told her she had always had an overactive imagination and if the truth were known, she was the one who came on to him. His final words to her were "I would never do that to you, Crystal. You have always been special to me."

Her issue then became one of self-doubt. Did she just have an overactive imagination? Did she actually come on to him?

He had always been kind. . . . How could she accuse him when he was always loving? Her roof-caving guilt intensified. I was alarmed as she slid back into the eating disorder accompanied this time with suicidal thoughts. She was saved from an immediate cave-in by a conversation she had with her younger sister. She learned the little sister had also been sexually fondled though not penetrated. The sister said, "He always told me I was special and that what he did was an act of love."

Those words of truth provided the paving stones Crystal needed to find her core self. She did not have an overactive imagination. Her brother had stolen her virginity and left her in a state of guilt-riddled confusion. Knowing the truth and where to place the blame was helpful to Crystal but oddly enough, her roof caved in anyway. The rubble of distrust, betrayal, and disillusionment needed to be dealt with before the roof could be repaired. It had been easier to blame herself than her brother. The cleanup was a year-long task.

But in the cleanup, Crystal learned to understand and use the "no" boundary word. It was not easy for her. Although the word is short and simple, it is sometimes excruciatingly difficult to say. Using it meant Crystal no longer attended family functions if her brother was present. She was still working her way through the cave-in rubble and was not strong enough to be around him. Her mother could not understand why Crystal said no to every family invitation. Crystal didn't know if she would ever talk to family members about her abuse. She doubted they would believe her anyway. Her brother was the "nice guy" whom everyone loved and admired.

Crystal came to think and believe the "no" boundary meant she need never again be up for grabs to be taken and used anytime, anywhere. She came to believe God placed a "no" on her soul to anyone who sought to defile her, His precious treasure, the work of His hands and the temple in which He lives.

Our counseling time basically ended with those soul-enriching affirmations. She moved to another state, got a job, and told me she was still cleaning up the rubble but feeling increasingly strong.

Sometimes the roof-nesters stay—and they don't notice the sags or take responsibility if they do. In a perfect world, Crystal's brother would have flown off and not Crystal. But she learned she has a God-given right to use the "no" boundary; that will help to rebuild her new roof.

The subject of boundaries and our right to establish them is sometimes confusing to those of us who believe we are to give to others and not concern ourselves about ourselves. The most brilliant, as well as biblically thorough, study on this subject is found in Dr. Henry Cloud and Dr. John Townsend's book entitled *Boundaries*. I strongly recommend it to you.

As you broaden your perspective on this subject, remember that everything about God is stated in His Word. He loves and cares for us as individuals. The decision to receive Christ is an individual choice; to honor our bodies as His temples is an individual choice; to set aside time for private prayer and worship is an individual choice. God does not see us as merely a clump made up of individuals. Each of us is called by name.

To commit ourselves to the needs of others must be a commitment that is balanced and prudent. When we overcommit, we become fatigued and overwhelmed. Saying yes can be Spirit-induced; so can saying no. Proverbs 22:3 cautions us with these words: "A prudent person foresees the danger ahead and takes precautions; the simpleton goes blindly on and suffers the consequences."

Roof Maintenance

1. Explain what a "no" boundary is. Do you have family members who do not understand that boundary?

2. Do you understand the "no" boundary? Why is it so hard to establish that boundary with a parent?

3. Do you agree "it is impossible to have healthy connectedness without knowing healthy separateness"? Talk about your efforts to be a loving but separate daughter to your parents.

4. Is it a sign of Christian maturity to always put the needs of others ahead of your own?

5. Discuss Proverbs 22:3: "A prudent person foresees the danger ahead and takes precautions; the simpleton goes blindly on and suffers the consequences." How does it apply to the way you live?

6

PLEASURE, ADDICTION, AND OUR ROOFS

What is your idea of pleasure? I recently asked that question of a number of my friends, all of whom are basically sane and stable. The answer I received the most frequently was to sink into a warm, relaxing bubble bath with a great book and a Do Not Disturb sign on the door.

Though I think the idea is pleasant, for me, the challenge of keeping my book dry and the water temperature constant is too troubling to be worth the effort. I prefer a warm shower. I'll read when I dry off.

I got a giggle reading about a unique bath invented in 1636 by an Italian, Doctor Sanctorius. It was called the "bath bag." The bather crawled into a large leather sack and had the top of the bag sealed around the neck like a collar. Hot water was then poured in through a funnel at the bather's shoulder. It washed over the body and down toward the feet where it drained out of a long spout. If the bather preferred a leisurely soak, the spout could be plugged. Certain models had watertight arms and gloves enabling one to read or write while enjoying a continuous cleansing flow. Dr. Sanctorius believed the principle advantage of his bath bag was that it allowed the bather to receive visitors while still maintaining modesty and decency. This solution for ridding the body of a day's worth of dirt and tension strikes me as a bit hairbrained. However, the idea of watertight arms and gloves has possibilities. But of course the problem of water temperature maintenance would still exist. Maybe one of the "visitors" could see to that.

Pleasure is one of God's gifts. Even so, from the Puritans to the Amish, Christians have historically felt a certain distrust of pleasure. There are some seemingly crabby verses that could support that distrust. Second Timothy 3:4 warns we are not to love pleasure more than God. Let me paraphrase a few others:

But she that lives for pleasure is dead while she lives.

(1 Timothy 5:6 NIV)

Traitors, heady, high-minded, lovers of pleasure more than lovers of God.

(2 Timothy 3:4 KJV)

You are a pleasure—a crazy kingdom, living at ease and feeling secure, bragging as if you were the greatest in the world.

(Isaiah 47:8)

If taken out of context, we might not believe pleasure is one of God's gifts. How could it be? If sounds as if pleasure and trouble go together. A friend of mine told me she was raised in a very strict and unforgiving faith culture. They said: "If you're smiling, you must be having fun. If you're having fun, you must be sinning. So don't smile!" That thinking implies smiling is the first step toward a moral cave-in.

As in all things, we want to maintain a balanced and thoughtful understanding of what the Bible teaches about pleasure. Consider the following verses:

. . . God, who richly gives us all we need for enjoyment.

(1 Timothy 6:17)

Whatever is good and perfect comes to us from God.

(James 1:17)

God intends that His good and perfect creation be appreciated by us; that it give us pleasure. I love that after each of God's creative acts recorded in Genesis, He stood back and "saw that it was good" (Gen. 1:10). He encourages us to see just how good! Seeing the grandeur of His creation gives me enormous pleasure. Edith Shaefer described the incomparable handiwork of Nature as "Eden's leftover beauty." It is there for us to enjoy and from which to derive pleasure. Give me a cup of tea and a comfortable chair, my pleasure from left-over beauty has no limit. It is a sweet way to worship the God who reminds me, "In [My] presence is fullness of joy; at [My] right hand are pleasures forevermore" (Ps. 16:11 NKJV).

Obviously Scripture is not telling us to avoid pleasure; it can be a call to worship. It does, however, encourage us to experience pleasure with disciplined common sense. It makes sense that we strive for balance in all we do. It's possible to exercise too much, diet too much, talk too much, talk too little, discipline too much, discipline too little, volunteer too much, volunteer too little, drive too fast, drive too slow . . . you get the point. For many people, the challenge is to keep pleasure in a state of balance.

There is a portion of the human brain scientists refer to as the "pleasure center." It is a part of the brain that reacts enthusiastically to chocolate, pizza, pasta, lemon meringue pie, and any other favorite food (or activity) that provides you with pleasure. But we need to keep an eye on the pleasure center because it loves the concept of "more." Remember, the "more is better" lie was concocted by the enemy of the soul. "More" keeps us craving and not satisfied. The enemy baits the hook with "more" and dangles it in front of the pleasure center and waits for us to swallow it. If we swallow it, we can lose our balance.

For example, one or two chocolate buttercreams may seem reasonable. The "more" hook swings by and then perhaps several more chocolate buttercreams also seem reasonable until the box is consumed and we feel nauseous as well as guilty. Are we doomed to forever devour multiple chocolate buttercreams because we swallowed the hook that lonely Friday night? No, but we'd better sit up and notice that hook because it never tires of dangling luring enticements. The lure may change, but the false promise that "more is better" will not change. That lie will apply to anything in our lives.

Here's the sobering truth about the pleasure center: It is where the enemy hangs out. It's where the bait is stored and the hooks are sharpened. That does not make the pleasure center evil; it reminds us the enemy will take good and turn it into evil if given the opportunity. There was nothing evil about Eden's apple. It became an instrument of evil because God forbid eating it. Disobeying God was the baited hook, not the apple.

Here's one of the ways the enemy subverts our God-given pleasure center with the "more" hook: we love to be thrilled! There is a certain "high" that comes with being thrilled. We love to watch death-defying trapeze artists, a championship football game tied with ten seconds to go, souped-up race cars zooming at 150 miles an hour, or an Olympic swim competition where the American wins by a fingernail. Those are perfectly legitimate highs. We can, however, become addicted to thrills. Why? Because thrills produce a high. The high itself is not evil, but the "more" search can lead to evil. Proverbs 21:17 from *The Message* translation states: "You're addicted to thrills? What an empty life! The pursuit of pleasure is never satisfied."

The enemy knows the pleasure pursuit is never satisfied. That's why, if we are not vigilant, his "more" hook will work. He also knows the "more" pursuit can produce addictions. It can be a heartbreaking cycle and one in which balance can tragically be lost.

Let's take a minute to consider just what happens in the

pleasure center that produces the much-sought-after high. There are two key neurotransmitters in the brain: endorphins and dopamine. Those secretions have much the same molecular structure as morphine. When a substance (drugs, alcohol, or any other addictive stimulation) connects with the pleasure center, toots and whistles go off! Stimulation of the center causes the receptors on the neurotransmitters of brain cells to multiply. So when the addictive substance wears off, the newly created receptions need more. If they don't get more, the pleasure center is out of balance because more of the addictive substance is needed to produce the same high. That "more," if not satisfied, creates cravings.

Cravings require the pleasure seeker to find new and different ways to increase the brain's production levels of dopamine or endorphins. For the emerging alcoholic, that may mean switching from beer to wine and wine to hard liquor. In the case of the drug user, it may mean switching from marijuana to cocaine, coke to crack or methamphetamines.

So how does one know if they're addicted? It is not only craving more, it is devoting oneself habitually and compulsively to getting it. That means the addicted person's world revolves around one pursuit only: getting high and maintaining it. Sadly, the roof will cave before long because the pleasure seeker is not maintaining the high. Addiction usually precedes a cave-in. Why does a person reach the point of caring only for the high and not for the roof?

I'll never forget the look on her face as she sat in my office saying, "I've lost everything . . . my marriage, my children, my friends, and, I'm sure, God as well." She was still a pretty lady at age fifty-one, but the effects of her alcoholism showed on her slightly mottled skin and in her faded blue eyes. Her husband had pastored a number of churches, always managing to stay ahead of the rumors that his wife frequently appeared inebriated at church functions. Her two children did not bring friends home from school because she was usually passed out on the couch by three o'clock in the afternoon.

After the two boys went off to college, her husband, weighted down by her inability to function, resigned from the church, filed for divorce, and moved to another state. "They all did what they could" she said, "but I've been what you call down-and-out for ten years." She was a court-appointed client. To avoid jail time, the judge demanded she enroll in a twelve-step program as well as weekly counseling. I knew the judge's wife and suspected she was personally paying for the counseling as well as facilitating attendance at AA meetings. The judge's wife was a recovering alcoholic herself, a committed believer in Christ and determined her years of alcoholism would serve a redemptive purpose in the lives of those whom

God placed in her path. My new client was hopefully on that redemptive path.

Let's attempt an answer for the earlier question, "Why does a person reach the point of caring only for the high and not for the roof?" There are a number of factors to take into account in answering that question, but the bottom line answer is they don't care. They don't care enough for their spouse, children, or friends to admit their addictions and seek help. They don't care enough that they have lost their reputation and the loving support of others. They don't care even when their roofs cave in. They have reached the point of caring only for feeding their cravings and maintaining their highs.

How does anyone come to the place of losing everything without even caring? How can that be? This totally out-of-balance pleasure seeker cared at one time, but that is the tragedy of sliding from balanced pleasure to totally out-of-balance pleasure. Everything, including caring about anything, is lost in search of the preferred and new necessary high.

But addiction of any kind serves a crucial function—it distracts from pain. All addiction is about distracting the user from feeling pain. That pain may be current or buried deeply beyond conscious knowledge, but pain drives the addiction. The victim thinks, *Those feelings are so overwhelming, threatening, and persistent, I cannot cope with them.*

At this point, the ever-watchful enemy baits the hook that says, "You don't have to cope with that pain. Here, try this . . . use this . . . you will feel better immediately." If the hurting person swallows the bait, they are hooked into a distraction that produces, "I no longer care."

The best thing that could have happened to my new client was her roof caving in—twice. Though she lost her marriage, family, and reputation in the first cave-in, she benefited more from the second one. Her husband left her with a car as well as a small apartment for which he paid the monthly rent. When my client hit a child on his bicycle and was arrested for drunk driving, her remaining roof caved in, joining the rubble of the first one. It was then she decided to make a choice. "I can continue not to care and live with the consequences of that choice, or I can decide I want to get well. To get well I have to admit my life is totally unmanageable."

Alcoholics Anonymous (AA) believes it is easier to help alcoholics when they "hit bottom," or with our metaphor, when the roof caves in. It's then that their lives are so shattered and broken they are forced to make a choice to work through the pain of what caused the addiction. Was there a solution for my client? Absolutely. God had never removed His hand from her life or His love from her soul. But it was a long, hard journey for her and the roof repair was slow.

I am an ardent supporter of twelve-step programs that insist on personal accountability and group encouragement. I am also an ardent supporter of counseling; a place one goes for increased understanding of why and how the pleasure center got so destructively out of balance. It's also a place to learn why there was a particular vulnerability for the personally baited hook the enemy knew to dangle in front of his victim. Understanding can give clarity but it cannot heal. Only God can heal. As one acquainted with and trained for the challenges presented by emotional imbalance, I have to agree with Psalm 140:7 that the sovereign Lord alone is our deliverer. Mental health workers provide an invaluable service for roof casualties but God does more than provide a service. Isaiah 43:11 dogmatically states, "I, even I, am the Lord and apart from me there is no savior" (NIV).

My alcoholic client came to realize that God had never left her and never condemned her. It was that tender hard-core truth that daily enabled her to persevere on her redemptive path and determine her roof was worth fixing. She also had to realize healing is a lifelong journey not a onetime event. That is a tough reality to accept.

So what are we saying in this chapter? God created us to experience pleasure that is found in Him and authored by Him. The enemy, ever at odds with God, is committed to the task of distorting the pleasure center by making it a never-ending source of lies and deception. His goal? The physical, moral, and spiritual cave-in of every one of God's people. His method? The baited hook-lie stating "more is better." When we take the hook and swallow the bait we inevitably lose our balance.

What are we to do to maintain our roofs and restore our balance? Be vigilant as we enjoy the pleasure center and be reminded:

> Give all your worries and cares to God, for he cares about what happens to you. Be careful! Watch out for attacks from the Devil, your great enemy. He prowls around like a roaring lion, looking for some victim to devour. Take a firm stand against him, and be strong in your faith. (1 Pet. 5:7–9)

Roof Maintenance

1. In what ways do you maintain a balance between the experience of God-created pleasure and disciplined common sense?

2. How do you apply Proverbs 21:17 to your desire to live a balanced life: "You're addicted to thrills? What an empty life! The pursuit of pleasure is never satisfied" (MSG).

3. How does the enemy of your soul use the lie "more is better" to throw you out of balance?

4. What is the major attraction of addiction? It serves a purpose—what is that purpose?

5. What do you understand about your "pleasure center" located in the brain? Is it necessary to understand it? Why?

7

CHILDREN AND PORNOGRAPHY

R ecently I was chatting with some friends about what era we would like to live in other than the present. One friend thought she would prefer the era of Charles Dickens with the afternoon ritual of tea by an open fire beneath a cozy thatched roof. Another friend opted for the pageantry and fashion of an Elizabethan court where the train of her long dress would be carried by eager attendants.

But the suggestion of a little house on the prairie era prompted the greatest conversational intensity. "Why would you choose that era? Life was filled with hard times: crop-destroying locusts, clothes that itched, husbands who rarely talked, and relentless meal preparation at the mercy of a woodstove and, possibly, no chocolate!"

"But," she said, "sometimes I long for a simpler life; one without cell phones, the Internet, and television. I would love just to sit with my family each evening and talk or not talk . . . just be in the same room with no distractions."

I expressed concern that, were I a little-house-on-the-prairie person, I might be expected to knit or sew poorly fitting, itchy clothes or sweaters sporting multiple drop-stitches. My mind drifted back to the memory of my years-ago effort to master knitting. I was pregnant with our first child and somehow it seemed appropriate that I be found knitting in a corner, tending to my ever-increasing girth to the melodic clicking of knitting needles. However, all I seemed able to do was knit squares. That Christmas I gave my sister-in-law Marge ten of my squares and told her they were washcloths. I also included little "dry clean only" labels on each. (That memory still gives me a giggle.)

Was there really greater simplicity and closer family ties during the little-house-on-the-prairie era? In spite of my conviction (I would have made a lousy prairie wife and mother), I think my friend is right. Today's era of technological advances is sobering to me, not only because I am a tech moron but because I also know how those advances can be used for evil. Actually, I am more than sobered. At times, I'm afraid. There well may be wisdom in preferring the era of simplicity without cell phones, the Internet, and television. Let's talk about that.

In the early years of this decade, marketers and advertisers were having difficulty getting their messages of "Hey! Buy this!" to people. Their solution? Recognizing that sex sells, commercials, slogans, and store "brands" have become increasingly sexually explicit, and now the media pushes the limits as well. What was at one time considered unthinkable is now excused as a matter of personal choice. Our culture has become desensitized to sexually explicit advertising, television, and movies. A new generation is rising. They have been fed by not only inappropriate sexual content in the media, but now the availability of Internet pornography.

What scares me even more is the availability of sexual content or pornography over cell phones. The National Coalition for the Protection of Children and Families estimates it has become a $2.1 billion business. Teens and preteens have the availability of wireless Internet access. They can privately access pornographic pictures and video from mobile devices at any time and from anywhere. With the emergence of MySpace,

You Tube, and Facebook, over one hundred million users have learned how to upload and share digital images for anyone who chooses to click on. Shot with web cams and cell phones with built-in cameras, uninhibited teens can share their own sexual images and messages with a network of friends and classmates. It can be done as quickly as it takes to walk from English class to social studies.

How will all this explicit and easily available sexual information affect the development of our young people? How are their values being reshaped? Research on these questions reveals alarming answers. Not only are our young people seeing more, they are doing more. Many of them do not believe there is anything wrong with sexual touching and fondling. There is, in fact, a high percentage who believe that not only are touching and fondling are acceptable, but so is oral sex. They think that form of expression is not sex; intercourse is sex. By not "doing intercourse" they avoid diseases, pregnancy, and unwanted commitment. Oral sex is easy, quick, and safe; there's no need for a room or backseat of a car. More and more preteens are also engaging in oral sex. A principal of an elementary school in my neighborhood told me the yard supervisors need to be alert to more secluded areas of the playground in order to monitor this "new" acting out of sexual behavior during recess.

With these kinds of tween and teen sexual experiences, we are going to have a generation of young people who have no idea how to have a genuine relationship. Their sole preoccupation will be to find a person willing to become a sexual object solely for the purpose of personal gratification. A prerequisite for a relationship then will be, "Does he or she satisfy my sexual need?" not "Do I want to 'love, honor and cherish'?"

I cannot tell you how I hate writing about all this. It is horrifying and appalling to see a profit-driven industry making money off the stolen innocence of our kids. But must we be the helpless victims of this wave of explicit trash that encroaches upon our children and pollutes their minds? We answer that question with a resounding no! Our voices need to be raised in vocal opposition to companies that "sell sex." We need to write letters, boycott products, and work to educated a naive public to the fact that we have a life-threatening epidemic going on. We need to face the facts, educate people about the facts, and then work to change the facts.

Quite frankly, I am one who has needed to be educated about the facts. Until I began researching this topic, I was certainly troubled by the explicit sexual advertising all around me but totally clueless about cellphone porn availability. I was also clueless that even grade school kids are experimenting with oral sex. Those facts totally got my attention. We, as a society that loves and cares for our young people, need to become informed.

When we are ill informed, we can be compared to what scientists call "dead zones." They, however, are not referring to inappropriate sexual behaviors but instead to a scientific reality threatening our coastal ecosystems. Dead zones are areas of the ocean with oxygen levels so low marine life can barely survive. Those zones have doubled every ten years since the 1960s as a result of a runoff polluted with nitrogen-rich crop fertilizer. There are now more than four hundred such zones stretching from the Gulf of Mexico to the Black Sea.

Unless we face a few unpleasant facts about what is happening to our youth culture, we are all going to be living in a dead zone, unaware that "runoff pollution" is threatening their survival.

In addition to raising our voices in opposition to the sex-sellers sliming their way into the minds and souls of our kids, we need to begin focusing specifically on individual young people. This challenge is not only for parents but for anyone who fears "dead zones" in our society. One of the keys to community survival is community volunteering. The possibilities for service and involvement are endless. The same potential exists in the church community. We can't do it for all, but we can do it for some. Together, we can do it for many.

What is the "it"? The "it" is educating individual kids about their own dignity and value. They must learn no one's body is simply an object or a commodity to be exploited and used for cheap sexual recreation. The body is to be treasured, guarded, and defended against anyone who lacks respect for its God-given value.

And the "it" is also educating young people that the word *no* may be the most important word in their vocabulary.

"No, you may not touch me."

"No, I will not touch you."

"No, I will not change my mind."

Many interviews with "no-saying" kids reveal they are more highly respected by their peers than the "yes-saying" kids. The no-sayers may not be invited to as many parties, but they can stay away knowing they are maintaining their dignity, value, and reputation. The guilt and shame that rapidly layer onto the souls of the yes-sayers is heart breaking. There is a solution for that: the word *no*.

And the "it" is also to teach a moral ethic set up by the God of the universe who states that ethic clearly in Scripture. The body houses the Holy Spirit, who enters our interior being the moment the decision is made to receive Jesus as

Savior. First Corinthians 6:13 says, "Our bodies were not made for sexual immorality. They were made for the Lord, and the Lord cares about our bodies."

> All sexual activity outside of marriage is immoral according to the Bible: "Run away from sexual sin! No other sin so clearly affects the body as this one does. For sexual immorality is a sin against your own body. Or don't you know that your body is the temple of the Holy Spirit, who lives in you and was given to you by God? You do not belong to yourself, for God bought you with a high price. So you must honor God with your body" (1 Cor. 6:18–20).

To realize that dead zones in our society may also exist in our church youth groups and even in our own homes is heart wrenching. Some think the Old Testament prophet Jeremiah can sound a bit "over the top" in his expressions of emotional anguish, but I "fell upon" several verses recently that seem appropriate for this discussion. We need to be a bit more "over the top" in our reactions to the soul pollution occurring in our society and encroaching upon our homes. We are admonished to: "Listen, you women, to the words of the LORD. . . . Death has crept in through our windows and has entered our mansions. It has killed off the

flower of our youth: children no long play in the streets."
(Jer. 9:20–21).

Those words from Jeremiah are directed to all of us who wish to avoid a roof cave-in. So armed with the call of Scripture to come to the rescue of our kids, we will take a stand against the soul pollution originating in sexually explicit advertising and porn sites. We will educate ourselves, our communities, and our churches. And we will focus on our kids who need individual education, guidance, and a consistent, loving presence.

But what about those of you who feel the roof has already caved in? You have discovered that your kids or the kids of those you know and love are indeed "dabbling" around with porn sites on the Internet and on cell phones. What do you do?

Let me back up to nearly forty years ago when I discovered Raquel Welch under the bed of my then five-year-old son, Jeff. I was performing my usual domestic duties when my vacuum cleaner tried valiantly to suck up a large piece of paper partially sticking out from the under side of Jeff's bed. Turning off the vacuum cleaner, I bent down and pulled out a life-size poster of the beautiful and voluptuous Raquel. I was stunned. "Why would my darling, sweet, and surely innocent little boy of five have this poster under his bed? He's a baby!"

I called Ken at work, and though he didn't say it, I sensed he thought his young son was showing good taste in women. The whole poster thing totally unraveled me. I was not sure how to handle it. We agreed I would "chat" with Jeff when he came home from kindergarten—KINDERGARTEN!

After two Mystic Mint cookies and two slices of apple, I asked Jeff if he would mind telling me about his Raquel Welch poster.

"Well, I think she is really pretty."

"What is pretty about her?"

"She has beautiful eyes and a beautiful face. I love to look at her."

"Do you think she should be wearing a blouse with a higher neckline?"

"Oh no, I think the blouse is perfect. It goes with her eyes."

"Were you hiding the poster. Is that why it was under the bed?"

"Well, actually, I wasn't sure you would like her eyes as much as I do."

Obviously this conversation about Raquel's eyes was going nowhere. I was stumped. *Surely it's too soon to talk about purity and how the eyes can open the door to impurity. Surely it's too soon to talk about how the mind opens up to impure thoughts that are hard to get out of the mind. Surely I don't need to explain God's standard of purity and that He tells us to be careful about what we see because we'll want to see more and more.*

I truly felt as if I was stumbling around in the dark, not sure what to say or how much to say. Jeff addressed my discomfort by suggesting I could have Raquel Welch under my bed instead of his if I wanted to. I suggested she not be under anyone's bed. He hopped off the kitchen chair and said, "Whatever you want, momma, is fine with me." He then sauntered out the door to play with Tommy who lived next door. I couldn't help wondering if Tommy had anyone under his bed.

Ken and I discussed it all when he got home from work. We had wondered if it was time for the "father-son chat" but Ken decided it might be too soon. I wasn't sure. From that point on, I became a snoop. I kept tabs not only on who might be under the bed but on who might be in the dresser drawers or closets. (I believe parents need to snoop . . . the information you reluctantly discover may save your child from serious trouble.)

When Jeff was nine, he received a letter in the mail addressed to "Mr. Jeffrey Meberg." The return address was *Playboy* magazine. Of course I opened it—that was effortless snooping. To my horror, the letter thanked Jeff for the interest he had shown in "Boom-Boom Dip Stick," their February bunny of the month. They regretted they would not be able to supply her mailing address but appreciated "Mr. Meberg's" interest. Obviously, the time for the "chat" had arrived.

Incidentally, it turned out I should have snooped at Tommy's house instead of mine. His dad had a subscription to *Playboy* magazine. Tommy regularly snuck the magazines out of the house to a little "bush fort" he and Jeff had constructed. There they did conscientious study of "bunny eyes."

Our goal for the chat was not to shame Jeff but to educate him. Ken talked to him about how normal it is to look at pretty women, but that looking at pretty women with little clothing can produce impure thoughts. Those impure thoughts are dangerous because the main sexual organ in the body is the brain. Once the brain is engaged it sends messages to the body, which it is all to happy to receive and act upon.

Jeff interrupted and said, "Hey, Daddy, I wrote one letter to one bunny; I don't think my brain had anything to do with it!" This conversation seemed to put an end to Jeff's overt interest in sexually explicit materials. It helped to have Tommy's mom cooperate in the removal of *Playboy* magazines. I would like to think that period of time was "boys being boys," but I know too much now to be casual about these experiences. Once the seeds are planted in a child's mind, there is reason to be prayerful and watchfully concerned.

For those of you who have experienced a cave-in more serious than mine, I'll suggest a few "what to do" ideas and then we'll discuss them:

1. Confront—wait until you are calm.

2. Be gentle but firm.

3. Do not use shame.

4. Do not accept denials or blaming.

5. Insist your child accept personal responsibility.

6. If cell phones or computers are used for sexual contact, ban them for a period of time.

7. Emphasize it is the behavior that is inappropriate, not the person.

8. Explain that inappropriate sexual behavior is sin.

9. When it appears genuine, have your child confess that sin to God.

10. Teach God's forgiveness of all sin.

The most crucial part of this "to do" discussion is to pray for and appeal to your child's desire to be pure. All the rules in the world will not cure the sinful inclinations of the human heart. So as you go through this suggested list, teach the biblical moral ethic. Your child needs to choose a cleansed heart, which will in turn produce reformed behavior. The words in 1 Corinthians 6:13 and 1 Corinthians 6:18–20 can be a beginning platform for your discussion. And, as stated earlier, your child needs to understand that a pure relationship does not include sexual behavior until after marriage. Your child needs to learn that a pure relationship is one of mutually honoring and cherishing one another's entire being, body and soul.

Now of course we know the toughest consequence to your child's inappropriate behavior is to take away the cell phone. The inevitable question will be, "When can I get it back?" I suggest saying, "You can earn it back." How? A contract. Here's how it works:

1. Have your child sign and date a pledge agreeing to never use the cell phone for sexually inappropriate purposes. That pledge applies to anyone else's cell phone as well.

2. Have your child agree to weekly accountability conversations with you. (You decide who, what, when, and where.)

3. At the end of the accountability meeting, sign and date a new pledge "renewing the vows" of the previous contract.

4. Conclude your accountability meetings with prayer, thanking God for His love, forgiveness, and strength to make wise choices.

5. Continue these accountability and contract renewals for at least eight weeks, or as you see necessary.

6. Don't have a meltdown when your child blows it. Start over and hang in there.

I recommend this contract procedure for computer misuse as well. Your child will possibly grumble under such close scrutiny, but I guarantee this behavior boundary will bring relief. Too many young people struggling with their emerging sexual drives are confused and have the guidance of only their friends who are equally confused. Proverbs 29:15 assures us: "To discipline and reprimand a child produces wisdom, but a mother is disgraced by an undisciplined child." Proverbs 12:15 states, "Fools think they need no advice, but the wise listen to others." We agree we love our little "fools," but we also agree they need advice, which will result in wisdom.

Since writing this chapter, I'm increasingly coming to agree the little-house-on-the-prairie era is a preferable one in which to live. Throughout all of human history there has been sin availability, sin choice, and sin consequence. But never before have our children had such overwhelmingly available sin choices as those now on the Internet. Technological advances are a perfect example of how a good thing can be used for bad by the enemy who wishes the moral destruction of all human life. What better place to start that moral destruction than with our children? The technology is not evil; the perversion of it is evil.

What gives me hope as I sit here rocking on my prairie porch and knitting squares, waving at Ken behind the plow, Beth at my feet playing with a corn-shuck doll, and Jeff gathering wood for my stove, is God's promise to me, no matter what era in which I find myself:

The LORD looks down from heaven and sees the whole human race. From his throne he observes all who live on the earth. . . . We depend on the LORD alone to save us. Only he can help us, protecting us like a shield. In him our hearts rejoice, for we are trusting in his holy name. Let your unfailing live surround us, LORD, for our hope is in you alone. (Ps. 33:13–14, 20–22)

ROOF MAINTENANCE

1. Discuss what is meant by "The new sexual acting out by tweens and teens means we are going to have a generation of young people who have no idea how to have a genuine relationship."

2. To what degree are you aware of the sexually explicit nature of advertising in magazines, billboards, television, movies, etc.? What can you do to counteract this morally destructive climate?

3. Discuss the ideas in this chapter about the steps you can take if you discover pornography use by your kids.

4. What is your response to the caution for parents not to use shame in their discipline of children and pornography?

5. What kinds of encouraging words and behaviors do you think parents need to use with their kids?

8

SEXUAL ADDICTION

Pornography has fast become America's number one addiction. Many observers believe it has also become a number one addiction among Christians. That last statement gives many of us whiplash. How could that be? We tend to think Christians don't have addictions—they have Jesus. And then we think, *If Christians have addictions, they don't have Jesus. It isn't possible to have both, right?* It is possible to have both. Christians are forgiven, but their sin inclinations still can have mastery over their behaviors. What is going on and why? How can it be that so many high-profile Christian leaders have lost their way? Sadly, it is not only high-profile Christian leaders who have lost their way. It may be your Christian neighbor. It may be your Christian committee member, it may be your husband and yes, it may be the wife of any one of them—or it may be you. Because of the shame that accompanies sexual addiction, it is the most agonizing of them all. Needless to say, this is a huge cave-in event that is no respecter of roofs: it strikes both Christians and non-Christians.

Before we begin a specific discussion about sexual addiction, let's take a minute to understand how an addiction gets its start. We have already discussed the enemy's tactic of dangling the tantalizing hook, which inspires the desire for more. The desire for more is rooted in the pleasure center of the brain. When the pleasure center desire gets out of balance, the hook is swallowed and the drive for more becomes a pattern that can result in addiction. But why is a person vulnerable to the hook? Why are some people more likely to become addicted than others? We all love the feeling of a thrill and the high we experience from it. Why doesn't everyone swallow the hook that may ultimately produce addiction? Here's why.

Remember, addiction serves a function greater than the pleasure of whatever is on the hook. Addiction is about distraction from emotional pain. It keeps one distracted from feelings one doesn't want to feel, memories one doesn't want to remember, and losses one sometimes denies ever experiencing. Our ever-alert enemy takes all that into account and baits a tailor-made hook designed for our individual vulnerabilities.

All of us share an individual vulnerability in that we have all experienced losses with varying degrees of intensity. Loss of what? Connection. We were created for connection, and if for any reason that connection is lessened or totally lost, the human soul reacts with a soul-wrenching and primal fear. All loss is about abandonment.

In my book *Love Me Never Leave Me* I discuss the heart cry of all humanity, which is, "Please love me and please, please, never, ever leave me. If you leave me, I may not survive." When that heart cry is ignored, there springs then the potential for any addiction promising to distract from the pain of abandonment. It is the source of all our addictions, compulsions, and emotional distress. God's promise to "never leave us or forsake us" is the greatest soul-medicine available to the one reeling from abandonment.

In an effort to explain how it is so many Christians are suffering from sexual addiction, it is helpful to pinpoint the original abandonment pain. Knowing that will not necessarily eliminate the pain or the addiction, but it provides a starting place on the path to recovery. The path can lead to the healing of that pain or at least provide tools for managing it. It also invites the healing presence of a Savior who reminds us we are not alone and He was never indifferent to those experiences that originally hurt us.

Since we usually think sex addiction is a problem for men and not for women, we can be startled to realize it can cave in the roofs of women as well. A new book from Pure Life Ministries by authors Steve and Kathy Gallagher explores female addiction and declares it to be a crisis brewing in the church. They believe the church needs to create an atmosphere where women feel it's safe to come forward and admit their struggles. If that does not occur, the majority of them will remain in their addictions as well as their shame.

I have been heartened to read the story of a young woman who is a pastor's daughter, a Christian, and now one not only released from her addiction but helping others to do the same. She tells what happened to her and explains the shock of realizing the part her abandonment issues played in launching her addiction.

When Donna was three years old, her mother died. Her grief-stricken father buried himself in his ministry duties, usually not coming home until late at night. One of her caretakers was a twenty-year-old man, a member of her father's church who became a substitute father figure. He was never too busy to spend time with her.

From the age of five until she married at the age of

twenty, he was sexually inappropriate with her. Because he was loving, gentle, and never coerced her, it never occurred to Donna his behavior was inappropriate. It felt like love to her—a connection she desperately wanted. At the age of fifteen, when intercourse became a part of the relationship, she began to feel guilty. As a preacher's kid, she had never missed church or Sunday school. Well schooled in Scripture, she realized she was participating in a sinful act, but didn't want to stop. He had been her loving rescuer, the one who never left her. The sin could not be his fault—it must be hers. She chose it; she needed it. She concluded that she must be a very bad person with very bad needs.

It is typical of children to take the blame for adult mistakes, as well as to blame themselves for "bad" circumstances that would not have happened if "I were not a bad person." With her child logic, Donna blamed herself for her mother's death as well as her father's unavailability; if she were not a bad person, her mother would not have died and her father would have chosen to be with her.

One of the characteristics of addiction is that life becomes unmanageable and beyond personal control. The recognition and agreement of that unmanageability is the first step to recovery. After three failed marriages, all to "nice Christian men," Donna realized she was a failure as a mother, a wife, and a Christian leader. She was compulsively drawn to Internet pornography and multiple affairs. Her third husband told her the marriage was finished; he wanted nothing more to do with her. Though she had been repeatedly unfaithful in all her marriages, his words merely highlighted the imprint branded in her soul as a child: "You are a bad person with bad needs; no one wants or loves a bad person."

It was not until Donna was in counseling that she realized the depth of her abandonment pain. Understandably, she had turned to whoever was there to comfort her, even if that comfort included inappropriate fondling. But her need was not her fault; the pleasure from fondling and subsequent intercourse was not because she was a bad person but because she desperately needed human connection. She had become the object of bad behavior from a person who took advantage of her vulnerability. When Donna became an adult, she then had to take responsibility for her adult behavior that was destructive and sinful. That is another step on the path to recovery.

Donna became desperate and determined to reclaim her life, which had been wrenched from her as a child. Through sensitive and skilled counseling, Donna grieved her losses and came to understand how she had come to use sex as an escape from her feelings of sadness, guilt, and shame. Since depression usually accompanies sexual shame, Donna bene-fited from medication, which stabilized her emotions and facilitated her recovery.

Also crucial to Donna's recovery was a twelve-step group for sexual addiction. It was there she found nonjudgmental acceptance as well as structured accountability. The twelve steps led Donna through the methodical process that focuses on addictive behaviors and how to regain control of a life that has become uncontrollable.

Is addiction inevitable if there is only casual interest in the sexual content of magazines, books, movies, and television? It is not, but it may be dangerous; that is enemy territory. It is between you and your desire to honor God that needs to determine the degree to which you interact with sexual media content. It is also important to understand the degree to which you need mood-altering experiences used to distract you from losses in your life. All addictions have their root in abandon-ment losses.

Michael Leahy, in his excellent book *Porn Nation*, chroni-cles his journey from the seemingly innocent curiosity of looking at porn flash cards as a junior-high boy to his helpless addiction to anything pornographic later in life. The porn cards provided an emotional escape for him. He was the tar-get of bullies at school and an abusively raging father at home.

The sexual feelings from looking at the cards distracted him from the absence of a safe school and loving home. Years later, still using pornography as his "safe escape" from feelings, he discovered Internet porn. Many experts refer to it as "the crack cocaine of sexual addiction." Michael was hooked. Only after losing his marriage, two sons, and lucrative career did he hit bottom. Recognizing that his life was totally unmanageable, he sought help. That help was found in a twelve-step program, private counseling, and a church that did not shun him.

Nate Larkin, a former pastor, tells his story of addiction and recovery in *Samson and the Pirate Monks*. He, too, realized through counseling that his boyhood abandonment set him up emotionally for addiction. His mother had periodic episodes of mental health breakdowns—one of them so severe, she was taken from her eight children and placed in an institution.

Nate's father was unable to provide and care for eight children by himself, so they were dispersed to the homes of friends and relatives. The children were told only that "Mom is sick but she is going to be OK." For over a year Nate and his siblings waited for her to come home. Ultimately the children were told their mother had died. That was all the information Nate had until he was sixteen years old, when his dad finally told him his mom had committed suicide.

With Michael Leahy, Nate Larking, and countless other men and women, the pornography available on the Internet plays into the need of persons searching for distraction from emotional losses and does so with relative anonymity. Persons who would not risk being seen buying a pornographic magazine can, in the privacy of their homes, have access to any kind of porn-sex imaginable. Not only is there a degree of anonymity with Internet porn, there are one thousand new pornographic Web sites that enter the superhighway daily. This provides an endless array of "more."

How does a person know if he or she is addicted? For men, isn't it just "boys will be boys," and for women, "they just love the feelings of romance"? You know addiction has set in when sexual curiosity and interest turn to sexual need that is no longer under personal control. The desire for more and the vain effort of satisfying the more becomes a lifestyle. The bottom-line symptom: "I can't stop myself. No matter the consequences, I must have more."

So how do we repair the roof that cannot bear up under the weight of sexual addiction? On page 118 I list some great referral books that can be enormously helpful in walking you through the stages of repair work. But I am also including some steps to consider that may encourage you to believe roof repair is possible in spite of the damage:

1. It Can't Be Done Alone.

We are created for connection and to face the challenges of addiction. You must have another human being walking your path with you. It is impossible to recover in isolation.

2. There Must Be Accountability.

Not only is it crucial to have someone walking your path with you, recovery must involve accountability for what is happening on your path. The best place for personal connection and personal accountability is found in a twelve-step program. More and more churches are realizing the need to provide a place, like a twelve-step program, where it's OK to have problems and it's OK to bring those problems to a place where there is love, support, and accountability without shame.

3. Personal Counseling Provides Understanding About Emotional Pain Leading to Addiction.

A twelve-step program is meant to provide a framework whereby addictive behavior is confronted and changed. Counseling provides the opportunity to work on the personal problems that led to addictions or that accompany the original addiction.

4. CHOOSE TO BE COURAGEOUS.

It takes tremendous courage to face life without the coping prop of addiction. It's the addiction that has helped you cope with the pain of your losses. It has become a way of life. Many fear there is no life apart from their addiction.

5. KNOW IT CAN'T BE DONE WITHOUT GOD.

Here's a great and encouraging truth found in 2 Corinthians 4:7–8:

> But this precious treasure—this light and power that now shine within us—is held in perishable containers, that is, in our weak bodies. So everyone can see that our glorious power is from God and is not our own. We are pressed on every side by troubles, but we are not crushed and broken.

You and I live in "perishable containers." We are all vulnerable to the invading forces of evil because of our "weak bodies." But we are also chosen to be cleansed and forgiven containers in which the "glorious power" of God enables us to resist being "crushed and broken." He gives to us "light and power" that shine within us. That is amazing grace!

A part of His amazing grace is that He uses people to be light and power in our lives. We were created for connection with God as well as connection with His people. In partnership with Him and those chosen to be our light and power, the roof will be repaired! Be encouraged—God wants that as much as you do.

ROOF MAINTENANCE

1. Why are some people more likely to become sexually addicted than others?

2. Does it make sense to you that abandonment is the source of all our addictions, compulsions, and emotional distress? How does that apply to your life?

3. Since female sexual addiction is a problem for women in the church, what kind of approach could your church use to address this challenge? How does that reality make you feel? Do you want to withdraw from the problem, or do you feel eager to be a part of the problem's solution?

4. How does one know if he or she is sexually addicted? What's the distinction between sexual interest and sexual addiction?

RECOMMENDED READING AND OTHER RESOURCES FOR RECOVERY FROM SEXUAL ADDICTION

Create in Me a Pure Heart: Answers for Struggling Women by Steve and Kathy Gallagher

A Biblical Guide to Counseling the Sexual Addict by Steve Gallagher

Healing the Wounds of Sexual Addiction by Mark Laaser

The Game Plan: The Men's 30-Day Strategy for Attaining Sexual Integrity by Joe Dallas

Every Man's Battle: Winning the War on Sexual Temptation One Victory at a Time by Stephen Arterburn

Porn Nation: Conquering America's #1 Addiction by Michael Leahy

Samson and the Pirate Monks: Calling Men to Authentic Brotherhood by Nate Larkin

The Life Recovery Bible

New Life Ministries (1-800-New-Life or www.newlife.com)

Woodmont Hills Counseling Center, Nashville, Tennessee (www.woodmont.org)

9

PREVENT
A MARITAL CAVE-IN

June 17, 1961, was the hottest day on record for the little town of Battle Ground, Washington. The Pacific Northwest rarely experiences temperatures exceeding 100 degrees, but the heat that day melted my wedding cake! It melted everyone in attendance; their love and loyalty for Ken and Marilyn exceeded their preference for the shade of trees. (I don't remember having air conditioning in those days. . . . However, I do remember we had motor-driven cars.)

As my pastor-father performed our wedding ceremony, I watched a bead of perspiration, originating from his forehead, make its deliberate way down the side of his nose, enter the crease line of his cheek, pause, double in size, and then slide into the corner of his mouth never to be seen again. I was mystified Dad did nothing about the sweat bead. As if unaware, he just let it trickle undeterred at a pace and destination of its own determination.

Though the sweat bead served as a welcome distraction for me, it also became a metaphor for what I was experiencing. The idea of marriage scared me and yet there I was, like the sweat bead, slowly making my way to a destination of its own determination. I was agreeing to "love, honor, and obey until death do us part." Would that marriage vow cause me to be swallowed, disappearing to a destination not of my own making? That was my fear; that was the fear that caused me to repeatedly break our engagement and postpone the wedding.

I was raised to believe marriage is a very big deal to God and not to be entered into lightly. I believed it then and I continue to believe it now. It's the fact that God places such an emphasis on the sacred holiness of marriage that caused me to feel insecure about my ability to live up to its high calling.

It was also my fear of being swallowed up, losing my identity, laying aside whatever I wanted to do in deference to what a husband wanted to do. I soon learned Ken had no intention of swallowing me up. He loved and took pleasure in my identity. To the degree possible, he supported my desires until death did indeed "do us part." By the same token, I supported him. It was a "give and take" relationship. God does not author a dictatorship in marriage, but a partnership. Ken taught me what partnership looked like.

God illustrated partnership in His original creation saying "that's good" after each addition made to Paradise. But after creating Adam, He said, "It's not good for man to be alone." It became good when Eve was created for Adam to be a loving companion and partner. It was then God's ideal was achieved. His ideal is a mutual union based on a pure and holy love that exists for a lifetime. But as biblical history teaches us and personal experience shows us, pure and holy love is an ideal lost in Eden. We work toward it, but achieve it briefly and fleetingly. Nevertheless, from Genesis to Revelation, God tirelessly speaks of the marriage relationship as His supreme illustration of love and partnership. Interestingly, God places Himself in the role of loving husband. or Him to do that may sound a "little out of the box" for some ears. Here are a few verses to refresh your memory.

> . . . for your Creator will be your husband. The LORD Almighty is his name!
>
> (Isaiah 54:5)

Come with me! I will show you the bride, the wife of the Lamb.

(Revelation 21:9)

Return home you wayward children, says the LORD, 'for I am your husband.

(Jeremiah 3:14)

Why does God refer to Himself as husband? He wants His beloved to know how to be a husband, so He set the example by modeling husband behavior to Adam. God meant for that modeling to be continued for all generations. What are some of these modelings?

1. God as husband thoroughly knows us.

2. God as husband loves us no matter what.

3. God as husband forgives us when we ask.

4. God as husband will never leave us.

Obviously, we women need to pay attention to God's model because those behavioral standards apply to wives as well. When both husbands and wives know, love, forgive, and stay with each other, the marriage bond reflects God's modeling.

We can see how marriage is God's showpiece relationship, so why is it that a relationship that matters to the heart of God seems at times to matter much less to the hearts of us? I don't think the majority of us think marriage doesn't matter, it's just that it's so hard. So hard in fact, I was scared to get into it. I was afraid I might, once having given my heart, find myself wanting to take it back.

I believe one of the reasons there are so many heart take-backs is we don't really understand the heart business. We don't always know what our heart truly wants and certainly can be clueless about what the heart of our spouse wants.

I'm sure I don't need to tell you the most common sentence heard in a counseling session is, "I don't understand him/her!" Who has not felt that way at some time with everyone in the world? Also, who has not muttered an unknowing and therefore unhelpful, "What's your problem?"

I can tell you what my problem is and I can guess what your marital problem is. We all want to be loved enthusiastically, accepted uncritically, and never fear we'll be left when "they" find out we are impossible to love enthusiastically and uncritically every minute of the day. The fact that God loves like that is a comfort, but He's not the one sitting wordlessly at my kitchen table! Are we then wanting too much? Of course. Our needs are like the Grand Canyon—

deep and wide. That's the first fact we must know about each other's hearts. It is impossible to fully fill the heart's Grand Canyon. Why? Our need for love is insatiable—we always want more. (That's why Satan's strategy works so well.)

What we need to know about each other's hearts is that they come with a huge cavity originally designed to be filled with God's never-ending, unfathomable, dependable, and uncritical love. In Genesis we read of God strolling Paradise in the cool of the evening, chatting amiably with His prized creation. They're enjoying each other's presence, loving one another tenderly with no thought of, *Am I good enough for you? Will you ever leave me?*

The sin of disobedience caused the most catastrophic cave-in ever experienced in human history. It changed the way our heart cavities are filled. The heart need is no longer met automatically and effortlessly. We have to choose the degree to which we want to partner with God and invite His filling of the heart cavity. It was human disobedience that ruptured the heart's fullness for all earthly time. It was human disobedience that birthed our need of more.

So what does all that Eden-knowledge have to do with our insatiable and needy hearts? What we need to know about each other's hearts is that humanly, we will never be able to fully fill the heart cavity; we are no longer perfect. We live in paradise lost. That being the case, we need help. God provides that by giving the God-as-husband model to follow.

As Adam, Eve, and God strolled through paradise, they talked. They talked for the purpose of knowing each other. Knowing was not something God the creator needed—He knew His beloved. But they did not know each other. They fell more deeply in love as they increasingly talked and became known to one another.

When you think about Adam and Eve talking, you have to wonder how much there was to say. Neither of them had mother issues to work through, the lingering resentment of a noncommunicative father, or the alcoholic uncle Buford who continually unsettled family gatherings. What was there to talk about? Their feelings! They talked about feelings. They must have been on sensory overload every single minute. "Adam . . . come here and see the colors of these irises," or "Eve, you have to see this lion who keeps licking my face." It is in our God-given nature to share our feelings. Our earthen vessels cannot contain them all. God, the husband model, illustrated with Adam and Eve the rewards of talking, listening, and sharing feelings. They shared with each other; God talked and shared with them. It was a partnership.

Most men would love talking about a huge lion that kept licking their faces. That's a straight-out fact that is easy to tell. (Of course, hard to believe, but that's beside the point.) However, those men might become uncomfortable if they had to not only report the lion experience but talk about what they felt about it. Questions like, "Did the lion cause you to feel panic?" "Did that panic remind you of any other time in your life when you felt panic?" "Would you like to talk about it?" Be prepared for, "Why is there no peanut butter chocolate fudge ice cream in the freezer?"

When a wife makes the simple statement, "We've got to talk," it strikes greater panic in most men than a lion's lick ever could. Why? Most men are not sure what they feel. At the risk of alienating every man on the planet, I'd venture that many men are more inclined to be hunters who want to come home to a clean cave and a good meal. Top that off with sex, and it's a good day. Anne Lamott vents a touch of frustration in her book *Operating Instructions: A Journal of My Son's First Year*: "Part of me loves and respects men so desperately, and part of me thinks they are so embarrassingly incompetent at life and in love. You have to teach them the very basics of emotional literacy. You have to teach them how to be there for you."

Studies devoted to the differences between men and women indicate women are better able to verbalize their feelings than men, but that does not mean men do not need emotional satisfaction. Some studies say boys are inherently little warriors who must live out of their primitive instincts. Others say we are living in an era of insecure men who have been so dominated by strong women they have retreated somewhere with the TV remote. We may never totally understand the many differences between the sexes, but we can understand the two sexes need to talk. When talk leads to understanding and understanding leads to acceptance, we've just laid the foundation for emotional connection. What is acceptance? It is "to believe in." When we, through conversation and understanding, reach the point of "believing" in each other, intimacy can follow. That's God's ideal.

So then, where do we start the knowing process that leads to emotional literacy and intimacy? If we didn't do much "knowing" during the dating process and skipped premarital counseling, we have to start at the very beginning of the knowing process. Perhaps we can learn something by observing the interactions of Bernadette and Lester.

We come upon them sitting at breakfast lingering over their second cup of coffee. They've been married for two days. Sex has been good; the marriage looks promising. The doorbell rings. Lester opens the door to a smiling man wearing a Bekins moving company shirt. A huge van is in front of the house.

Bernadette rushes to welcome the driver and instructs

him to unload the truck's contents into the garage. Lester is confused. "What are all those boxes? What's in them?"

"Oh Honey, it's just my stuff. I never go anywhere without my stuff."

Lester watches as the garage is filled with box after box of Bernadette's stuff.

When the empty truck pulls away Lester says, "How could you possibly have so much stuff?" Bernadette says, "I've been collecting it all since I was a child. That big box over by the water heater holds my unmet needs stuff. Then there's the very large box with my mother stuff. The father stuff box is next to it, and the really, really big box holds my shame stuff. The other boxes are important, too, but that stuff isn't as specific. They hold suggestions like what to do if you stop loving me or stop being nice to me."

Somewhat sheepishly Lester opens the door to another truck driver with a large van parked in front of the house. That truck arrived only an hour or so after the Bekins truck pulled away. Lester instructs the mover to take his "stuff" upstairs to the spare bedroom because the garage is already full.

Bernadette watches as Lester's labeled boxes are carted upstairs to be tucked away and out of sight. But one box startles her. It is labeled Never Trust a Woman and placed beside a huge box simply labeled Mother.

When Lester's boxes have been crammed into place and the door shut, Bernadette says, "Wow. I didn't know anyone else had as much stuff as I have! Do you ever look at your stuff?"

"Nope," says Lester, "I just drag it around with me."

"Me too," Bernadette sighs.

The reality is, all couples come together dragging their boxes of "stuff" with them. It's part of the marital package. Bernadette and Lester have carefully tucked away the most important "knowing potential" each needed to understand about the other. They avoided feeling their own hurt, pain, and confusion by not looking at it and certainly avoided sharing it with anyone.

It's time for them to open their boxes. If they never look, see and talk, there will be no understanding of each other beyond the shallow knowledge that Bernadette likes the color purple, prefers almonds to cashews, and is allergic to pine nuts. Lester, on the other hand, eats everything in sight, especially if it's battered and fried.

At Bernadette's urging, they began by looking into Lester's Never Trust a Woman box. Reluctantly he began to describe the childhood memories of his mother. She was demanding and unfeeling. If he did well, she never praised him saying only, "That's to be expected." She never cried or complained. She was merely an automation who did what was to be expected. Lester left home at the age of sixteen, lied about his age, and joined the army. While in the service he had two serious love relationships, but both girls cheated on him. Lester didn't let his heart go again until he met Bernadette.

She needed to know and understand Lester's "woman history." She needed to know his reluctance to touch (except for sex) came not from a rejection of her but from a basic lack of trust with human connection. She then needed to learn to be patient and sensitive to his occasional distancing from her. Knowing and understanding just that one box of Lester's "stuff" gave Bernadette an understanding of Lester's heart cavity and the degree to which it had never been filled. Knowing the contents of Lester's box made her love him more.

When Bernadette consented to open her shame box, Lester was stunned to learn Bernadette had experienced an abortion when she was sixteen. Her parents had warned her about her boyfriend and refused to allow them to see each other. But they met in secret, she became pregnant, and a girlfriend took Bernadette to a sleazy part of town for an illegal and cheap abortion. Her parents knew nothing about it but noticed she became unaccountably withdrawn and depressed. She graduated from high school and moved away. When Lester came into the coffee shop where she waitressed, his courteous reserve appealed to her. They married six months after meeting.

Opening the shame box was hard for Lester because it tapped into his issue of trust. Although they had never talked about it, Lester assumed Bernadette was a virgin. It was hard for him to learn she wasn't, but equally hard to learn she had aborted a human life. He admitted he might not have married her if he knew this history.

It was this very fear ("If you knew me, you'd leave me") that caused Bernadette to hesitate about opening her shame box in the first place. When she finally did, her fear was realized. Lester was not sure he could love her now that he really knew her.

They were both devastated; they desperately needed a competent counselor to come on the scene and walk them down their path of knowing, which could lead to either forgiveness or separation. It was during that process Lester came to understand the God-as-husband model. He learned that though God knows everything about us, He loves us no matter what. He forgives us and promises never to leave us. That was a tough model for Lester to follow.

He came to realize, however, that he had some work to do. He needed to do some forgiving of people in his past. He had never forgiven his mother for her cold indifference or the betrayal from his previous love relationships. He needed to seek forgiveness before he could give forgiveness. His heart had grown so protective, he feared he could become as cold as his mother had been. That was a sobering and unattractive realization.

The best thing that could have happened to Bernadette and Lester was to open their "stuff" boxes in each other's presence. It was risky to be so vulnerable and emotionally bare, but it forced them to seek much-needed professional help. Our early, unresolved stuff relentlessly clings to us like a static-saturated slip. All the "cling-be-gone" spray in the world will not release its determined hold on us.

When we face what we've avoided, forgiven ourselves and others for the things in our boxes, we can be free from the clinging stuff stored up in our boxes. With that freedom we can enter into courtship, where knowing each other needs to begin. As we gain confidence in each other's acceptance ("I believe in you"), the foundation is laid for the intimacy of a marriage relationship. Emotional literacy has been learned.

Bernadette and Lester did it all backwards but nevertheless, they reached the place of mutual forgiveness as well as a desire to fill as best they could the cavity in each other's hearts. Placed firmly in their spiritual consciousness was the inspiration of the God-as-husband model: knowing, loving, forgiving, and promising never to leave.

I have learned a lot about God, marriage, and life since June 17, 1961. I've learned that my life is not like the random trail of a sweat bead inching toward a destination of its own determination. There is nothing random about any aspect of my life, and I'm not in charge of its determination. God is. He is sovereign, not random. Therefore, my life path is sovereignly superintended by a loving God.

> "The LORD says, 'I will guide you along the best pathway for your life. I will advise you and watch over you.'" (Ps. 32:8)

Some of you may be in a marriage that does not feel like the "best path." You wonder how you can possibly believe God had anything to do with that path; everything on it feels so wrong. Be aware of the ways in which God is guiding you to places and persons who can come alongside you and help. That help may come from a friend, a pastor, marriage counseling, or all three.

I've also learned my greatest spiritual growth has sprung from my deepest human pain. Nothing in our lives goes to waste. All experiences, even a marital roof-cave-in, will ultimately work together for our good.

I've also learned to be patient about not knowing what God knows. He sees the big picture. I have to trust Him to take care of what I can't see. I also have to trust Him to ultimately make sense of what I do see. Your marriage may not make sense to you right now. Do what you can and trust God's "way" for the rest. Remember, your God-husband's way is to work out His plans for your life; God's faithful love endures forever (Ps. 138:8).

Roof Maintenance

1. Why does God refer to Himself as husband? Does that feel peculiar to you? In what way does it encourage you?

2. How do you respond to the illustration of the Bekins truck full of our "stuff"? Does that analogy make sense to you?

3. Do you know what stuff is packed up in your boxes?

4. Do you think a marriage partner needs to know what is in all your boxes? In other words, do you think secrets are okay?

5. When do you think it's okay to keep secrets and when is it not okay?

10

DIVORCE CAVE-IN

A man was leaving a convenience store with his morning coffee when he noticed an unusual funeral procession heading toward the nearby cemetery. A long, black hearse was followed by a second long, black hearse about fifty feet behind. Behind the first and second hearse was a solitary man walking a dog on a leash. Behind him, a short distance back, were about two hundred men walking in single file.

The observer couldn't control his curiosity so he respectfully approached the man walking the dog and said, "I'm so sorry for your loss. I realize this may be an inappropriate time for me to disturb you, but I've never seen a funeral procession like this. Whose funeral is it?"

"My wife's."

"What happened to her?"

"My dog attacked her."

"But who is in the second hearse?"

"My mother-in-law. She was trying to help my wife when the dog turned on her."

A thoughtful silence followed between the two men. Finally, the observer of it all asked quietly, "Can I borrow the dog?"

Its owner replied, "Get in line."

The frustrations of marriage provide endless numbers of jokes about the murderous instincts marriage can inspire. The irrepressible cartoon character Maxine offers her take on the topic: "Men are always whining about how we are suffocating them. Personally, I think if you can hear them whining, you're not pressing hard enough on the pillow."

Why is it the very relationship which so pleases the heart of God (and the one about which He talks lovingly throughout Scripture) should become the object of very funny but also tasteless jokes? And why is it we recognize murder is not an option but hope divorce is?

The reason is we want to stop the pain. Our human defense system is wired to react to and put an end to pain. Pain tells us something is wrong and it needs to be fixed. When it's fixed, the smart learner does not repeat that which first produced the pain. The child who touches a hot stove learns to avoid hot stoves in the future. The overeager chef learns to respect a sharp knife when his severed forefinger falls into the salad bowl. Self-preservation is an instinct. We need to understand and pay attention to that instinct. So then, can one plead, "I have to get a divorce to stop the pain, and if I don't do that I'll be ignoring my instinct for self-preservation"? Maybe . . . maybe you do.

Before we discuss the "maybe" let's discuss what kinds of pain drive people to the divorce court. I'll list the most common:

1. Infidelity

2. Abuse—physical, emotional, verbal

3. Addiction—pornography, alcohol, gambling, drugs

4. Incompatibility (irreconcilable differences)

Those who have sincerely placed their lives in the hands of a sovereign God need to know what Scripture teaches about divorce. Is there a "maybe" category? If so, what is it? On the other hand, those who wish to write their own bible can provide their own "maybe" category. They would first add a commandment to the original ten. Commandment Eleven would read, "Thou shalt not bore!" Based on the breaking of that commandment, people could rush to divorce courts all claiming to be suffering from "spousal fatigue," the inevitable result of boredom.

For those interested in studying the original languages of your self-written bible, the word *bore* can be interpreted "to induce drowsiness, apathy, dull headache, and loss of appetite." The advantage of knowing the linguistic implications of the word *bore* is that more people can then rush to the divorce courts. If the judge questions "spousal fatigue" as a justifiable charge, there's the more acceptable "irreconcilable differences" plea based upon the expanded understanding of the linguistic implications of the word *bore*.

So here's the bottom line: unless you write your own bible, "irreconcilable differences," which may include boredom, drifting apart, multiple unmet needs, loss of respect, and basic incompatibility do not provide grounds for divorce. It does, however, provide good reason to agree to resurrecting what feels like a dead marriage. How is that done? Stop searching for a divorce "maybe" and begin searching for ways to bring the dead back to life.

My highest recommendation to resuscitate the dead is a good marriage encounter weekend. The advantage of a weekend is the intense focus on what caused the marriage to get sick in the first place followed by intense focus on how to make it well. This is usually done in small groups whose members come to know each other, support each other, and cheer each other on to new life decisions. All of the group activity is superintended by a licensed counselor trained in ways to inspire insights that will lead the couples to healthy new thinking and behavior. Many couples decide against the divorce "out" and reclaim the ways in which their love can be rekindled and grow once again.

There are any number of good marriage encounter weekends, but the one I recommend the most highly is New Life Ministries (newlife.com). I am personally aware of the ways in which that biblically based encounter weekend works and the numbers of marriages that have literally risen from death to life.

After the jump-start a marriage encounter weekend provides, I recommend weekly counseling sessions to further facilitate new patterns of relating to each other. This is admittedly not an easy process and demands commitment, time, and energy. But it is cheaper and less painful than divorce. It's also God's intent.

So then, speaking of God's intent and recognizing irreconcilable differences are not grounds for divorce, let's talk about the "maybe" category. If you are well churched, you are familiar with the no-divorce-except-for-adultery verses. The bottom-line verse Malachi 2:16 states that God hates divorce. It goes contrary to everything He intended for His beloved. To God, marriage is more than a covenant between a man and a woman; it is a mystical union. Jesus described that union in Matthew 19:5–6: "'For this reason a man shall leave his father and mother and be joined to his wife, the two shall become one flesh.' So they are no longer two, but one flesh. What therefore God has joined together, let no man [*or woman*] separate" (NASB, addition mine). When a man and woman commit to "leave," "cleave," and then consummate their union in the one-flesh act of sexual intercourse, they are joined in a mystical union designed by God.

Because humanity could not live a pure life, that mystical union was not always honored, and the "maybe" category emerged. Jesus said that everyone who divorces his wife, except for the reason of sexual immorality, is wrong (Matt. 19:8). So Jesus is saying when the mystical union is severed by adultery, that severing creates the "maybe" release from the marriage bond. The reason I use the word "maybe" is because many persons hurt by infidelity choose methods designed to bring healing to the pain of betrayal. There again I recommend the New Life Ministries' weekend session or other equally qualified interventions designed to heal severed relationships.

There is another "maybe" category for divorce, which we first read about in Exodus 21:10–11. In essence, the book says everyone, even a slave wife, had three rights within marriage: the rights to food, clothing, and love. If these were neglected, the wronged spouse had the right to claim freedom from that marriage. These three rights became the basis of Jewish marriage vows. They were listed on marriage certificates discovered near the Dead Sea. The three provisions of food, clothing, and love were understood literally by the Jews. Each spouse had to provide emotional support for the other.

The foundation for Jewish and Christian marriage is to love, honor, and keep. These vows, together with a vow of sexual faithfulness, have always been the basis for marriage. If these vows promising to provide emotional and physical needs were not honored, according to Old Testament law, divorce was a rightful course of action.

Paul affirms those marriage stipulations in 1 Corinthians 7:3–5 when he said married couples owed each other love. He states in 1 Corinthians 7:33–34 that married couples owe each other material support. Paul did not need to say neglect of these rights was the basis of divorce because his Jewish audience understood that fact; it was stated on the marriage certificate. So then, anyone who did not receive emotional or physical support could legally seek divorce.

(If you wish to further research these ideas, I suggest you read David Instone-Brewer's excellent book *Divorce and Remarriage in the Church*.)

So let's talk about some specific instances when emotional support has been jeopardized in marriage. Let's first talk about physical abuse. When I say "physical abuse," I mean the bruised, broken bones, blackened eyes kind of abuse. Can we interpret 1 Corinthians 7 as lending support to those who want to divorce their abusing spouse? Is physical abuse an act that severs the marital bond and breaks the vow to "love, honor, and keep"?

Let's look at 1 Corinthians 3:16–17, which emphasizes the sanctity of our bodies that literally serve to house the Spirit of God:

> Don't you realize that all of you together are the temple of
> God and that the Spirit of God lives in you? God will bring
> ruin upon anyone who ruins this temple. For God's temple
> is holy, and you Christians are that temple.

This verse teaches us that when we receive Christ as Savior, the Spirit of God literally enters our interior being, cleanses it from sin and transforms it into the "temple of God" where He lives the rest of our earthly life. Because God is holy, our bodies become holy and we then are the "keepers" of that holy temple. Using extremely strong language, Scripture says God will "bring ruin upon anyone who ruins" this temple. What does that message say to the abuser? Expect ruin. What does it say to the one abused? Take care of the temple!

Taking care of the temple means no longer allowing it to be abused. What does that mean? If divorce does not seem sufficiently scriptural to you, then you need to separate yourself from the "temple-basher." Separating from the abuser means you have laid down a boundary that says, "Stop! You can never abuse this temple again!" If your boundary is ignored, stepped over, then your abuser must physically leave. If he won't, you must.

Scripture has many encouragements for us to separate ourselves from people whose behavior is destructive. Matthew 18:15–17 says we are to tell the offender about his sinful behavior; if that does not work, include several people as backups and present the sinful behavior again. Then take it to the church. If the person still won't turn from the sin, "treat that person as a pagan or a corrupt tax collector" (v. 17). 1 Corinthians 5:11 says, "You are not to associate with anyone who claims to be a Christian yet indulges in sexual sin, or is greedy, or worships idols, or is abusive, or a drunkard, or a swindler. Don't even eat with such people." The same message of our need to separate from ungodly behavior is stated in I Corinthians 5:13: "'You must remove the evil person from among you.'"

I think separation is also appropriate for the spouse experiencing the betrayal that accompanies certain kinds of addiction. Addictions like gambling, alcohol, drugs, and pornography are especially demoralizing to a spouse and destabilizing to the home, causing innocent children to feel confused and abandoned. There are times when a tough-love boundary is the only message that registers in the mind of an addict. "I'm leaving or you're leaving. You decide."

Let's go back to the God-as-husband model. When God told Abram to leave his home with all its secure familiarity, God made a covenant with Abram that promised a future nation. God and the Hebrew people became husband and wife.

When God first gave His bride the Promised Land, He made the terms of their marriage contract clear; it had specific boundaries. We read about them in chapter 28 of Deuteronomy. Those boundaries were: obey and be blessed or disobey and experience the consequence of being scattered "among all the nations from one end of the earth to the other" (v. 64). Throughout the Old Testament we see God as husband nurturing and protecting His bride, Israel. She, however, was not faithful. She worshipped other gods, rejected

His values, and pursued whatever sin she encountered. Because she did not honor her marriage vows and refused to repent, God as husband said He would no longer provide for her needs. The terms of the contract had been broken. He left her to her sin. Jeremiah 3:6–10 says God sent her away and gave her a "writ of divorce" (v. 8 NASB).

So how did the God-as-husband work for the unfaithful wife, Israel? It is still being worked out. You will remember God's husband-way is that He knows us, loves us, forgives us, and promises to never leave us. But nothing about the husband-love was passive concerning His rebellious bride. She has paid a heavy price for her centuries of sin choices. Each choice came with consequences. Without repentance and a genuine turning from that sin, the marriage contract is broken. However, there will come a day when repentance and a renewal of vows will restore the marriage relationship between God and His bride.

> "In that coming day," says the LORD, "you will call me 'my husband' instead of 'my master.' . . . I will make you my wife forever, showing you righteousness and justice, unfailing love and compassion. I will be faithful to you and make you mine, and you will finally know me as LORD."
>
> (Hos. 2:16, 19–20)

Following the God-as-husband model, which knows, loves, forgives, and never leaves is the ideal toward which we frail persons aspire. But abuse and addictions can humiliate and destroy the dignity of the human spirit. They can trample into the ground the struggling, faltering marital love to the point where finally it finds itself in a graveyard with the inscription Never Again. Is it possible to bring that love back from the grave? Yes, but only when genuine repentance occurs and behavior changes; then, and only then may the embers of that love slowly glow again. I've seen it happen. It will happen with God and His bride.

Though you may choose to leave, maybe divorce, you must choose to forgive. Forgiveness does not mean you reestablish the relationship that proved to be death producing. It means a God-enabled forgiveness is necessary to flush out the poison-pool in which unforgiveness languishes. A bitter and unforgiving spirit creates an unhealthy environment for your inner temple where you and God both live. Forgiving frees you to live in interior harmony.

Some of you may not feel God's permission to divorce for any reason other than that of adultery. It may feel as if Scripture is being stretched to include emotional and physical neglect mentioned in Exodus 21:10–11 and affirmed by Paul in 1 Corinthians 7. Jesus was so definitive, and since He did not explicitly state other behaviors allowing for divorce, you may therefore not believe you have biblical grounds. If indeed you fall into that category, I want to recommend the book *Redemptive Divorce* by Mark W. Gaither. I've never read a more sensitive, biblically balanced, and carefully researched book than this. He offers an out-of-the-box way of providing guidance for the suffering partner, healing for the offending spouse, and an amazing catalyst for marital restoration. Mark offers hope for all persons who are feeling they must choose between the lesser of two evils: divorce without sound biblical support or a life of unrelenting misery.

However you choose to heal, separate, or divorce, you must not walk that path alone. We are wired for connection. We need a counselor, coach, pastor, or group to encourage our inborn drive for self-preservation. Their presence assures you of survival, though it seems impossible at times. Take seriously the advice found in Ecclesiastes 4:9–12:

Two people can accomplish more than twice as much as one; they get a better return for their labor. If one person fails, the other can reach out and help. But people who are alone when they fail are in real trouble. And on a cold night, two under the same blanket can gain warmth from each other. But how can one be warm alone? A person standing alone can be attacked and defeated, but two can stand back-to-back and conquer. Three are even better, for a triple-braided cord is not easily broken.

I also strongly urge you to avoid any and all possible romantic attachments as you walk your recovery path. When the separated or divorced person rebounds into a new relationship, it serves as a welcome distraction from pain, but that distraction also serves as a blinder for understanding what went wrong in the marriage. We learn from mistakes. We need to know what our mistakes were that may have contributed to the death of the relationship. If we don't know and learn, we'll survive only to repeat the mistakes. That mistake may simply have been an inability to make a wise marital choice. Were there signals you missed during the courtship phase, or did you spot them but naively assume they would disappear after marriage? These are crucial questions for when you need answers.

Now is the time to devote yourself to an understanding of who you were, who you are now, and how you choose to be in the future. It's also a time for emotional and sexual abstinence. Stay with same-sex friends and groups. They can provide a steady, supportive, safe environment during this healing time. Claim the hiding place that David wrote of in

Psalm 32:7: "You are my hiding place; you protect me from trouble. You surround me with songs of victory."

ROOF MAINTENANCE

1. Why do you think so many people are shocked to find they "fell out of love" at some point after they married?

2. Do you think it is possible to "fall in love" again with the spouse for whom your heart has grown cold? Is there hope for rekindling the spark?

3. If a husband is an abuser, is that grounds for divorce?

4. Does an abused wife have to stay in the marriage when her life and the well-being of her children are in jeopardy? What does Scripture say about that?

5. Why is it important to avoid all romantic involvements during the divorce process?

11

DIVORCE CAVE-IN
AND THE KIDS

Two little boys, ages eight and ten, were always getting into trouble. If any mischief occurred in their town, everyone assumed the two boys were probably involved.

The boys' mother heard about a preacher in town who had been successful in disciplining children. She asked if he would speak with her boys. He agreed but insisted he see them individually. The agreement was that he would see the eight-year-old in the morning and the older boy in the afternoon.

The preacher was a huge man with a deep booming voice.

He sat the younger boy down and sternly asked, "Do you know where God is, son?" The boy's mouth dropped open but he did not say a word. He just sat there with a look of wide-eyed terror. The preacher repeated the question in an even louder voice, "Where is God?"

Still the boy made no effort to answer. The preacher raised his voice even more, shook his finger in the boy's face and bellowed, "Where is God?" With that, the boy bolted out of the room, ran home, and dove into his closet, slamming the door behind him.

When his older brother found him in the closet he asked, "What happened?" The little boy gasping for breath, said, "We are really in big trouble this time. God is missing and they think we did it!"

Now some of us "shrink types" might miss the joke and concentrate instead on trying to figure out what's gone wrong with those two little boys. Is mother divorced? If so, is she so overwhelmed that she cannot discipline her boys who have become town terrors? If she is divorced, where does the father live, or did he just disappear? If not, what is the visitation agreement? Do the boys understand it? How do they feel about all this? Who listens to their little hearts? We certainly hope they never see the "booming preacher" again!

For the sake of our discussion, let's assume the little

gentlemen in this story actually do represent two of the over one million kids who yearly become children of divorce. Let's also assume their "mischievous" behavior does indeed spring from their inner confusion as well as anger that dad is no longer living at home. It is typical for children to act out their pain in ways that are disruptive at home, school, and in the community. They don't know what to do with the pain, so they spread it around.

During my first year of teaching at Newhope Elementary in Garden Grove, California, I was totally overwhelmed and mystified by the behavior of one of my students named Jackson. He was eight years old and terrorized not only my classroom but the playground and, I later learned, his own neighborhood. He, too, could have been accused of "stealing God."

My principal, Dave, was a sensitive and competent administrator who suggested I call the mother of my little terrorist and have a conference. "Something's going on in that home, Marilyn. Jackson was never a problem last year." My heart dropped because I was sure my inexperience and age probably didn't help the situation. In fact, maybe it was my fault—I was only twenty-two. What did I know?

I came to know a lot, however, and Dave was right. A lot was going on in Jackson's home. As Jackson's mom, Cynthia, talked, she described how heartbroken she was when Jackson's father simply announced he did not love her anymore and wanted a divorce. Jackson was furious with his mother and blamed her his dad no longer lived with them. She was too tired after a day at work to fight with him, so he basically did whatever he felt like whenever he felt like it.

Dave had agreed to sit in on the last half of our conference, so after careful listening, together the three of us drew up what we hoped would prove to be a rescue plan for Jackson. (Actually, Dave did most of the work; I watched and learned a lot.) Here are the basic terms of that agreement:

1. Jackson had to have at least one weekly scheduled visit with his dad.

2. Jackson had to have regular and dependable hours: a time to come home, eat, play, and go to bed.

3. Cynthia committed to a daily "chat time" about anything either wanted to say.

4. Cynthia committed to never, ever say anything negative about Jackson's father.

5. Cynthia committed to a daily thirty-minute reading program with Jackson where he could read aloud to her.

6. Cynthia agreed to daily tell Jackson she loved him
   and to also praise him for either a behavior or a
   quality he possessed.

After these terms were agreed to, Cynthia signed the contract; Dave and I signed on as witnesses. We also agreed to have monthly progress reports where she would see me and tell me how it was going at home, and I would tell her how it was going at school.

There was a marked improvement in Jackson's behavior very soon after the "relief plan" was put in place. Cynthia said he sometimes argued against the new "rules" but also seemed to find security in knowing he couldn't just do anything he felt like. His reading began to improve and so did his sense of self-confidence. One morning while I was on yard duty, he asked if I thought he had "gorgeous blue eyes." I told him I'd always thought that. His response was, "That's what my mom keeps telling me."

Jackson still had occasional temper outbursts on the playground when he didn't get his way. And there were times when he would withdraw into moodiness in class, but recess generally pulled him out of it. Life was not perfect for this little man, and the loss of his dad was hard for him. But with renewed and consistent attention from his mom as well as structure in his home life, he was not the same boy I met the first day of school.

Since those days, important research has been done regarding the pain level of children of divorce. The question most frequently asked by divorcing couples is, "Are our kids going to suffer emotional damage if we divorce?" One respected researcher, after years of study, concluded that children of divorce are deeply traumatized and continue to suffer into adulthood. On the heels of that research came other published studies making the opposite argument. They maintain children of divorce recover quickly and are as emotionally stable as those from continuously married families.

How could serious researchers come to such contrary conclusions when studying the same subject? I think the truth may lie more in the middle and not at either extreme. I agree with a respected researcher, author, and university professor who believes it is a mistake to talk about divorce as being "good" or "bad" for children. He believes parents need to be aware of the pain that all children experience but also aware of the pathology that only a minority develop. In other words, divorce is *always* stressful and painful for kids; some are more at risk of developing emotional problems than others.

The encouraging word about all this speculation is that parents can eliminate a great percentage of the divorce pain by behaving in a civil and courteous way with each other. The greatest contributor to the pain of kids of divorce occurs when parents openly undermine, accuse, and blame each other. And even more damaging is when the child is dragged into the controversy and made to choose sides. That forces a child to label one parent good and one parent bad. Whichever choice the child makes, the fear of the child is, "I'm bad for choosing." That's why it is crucial neither parent bad-mouths the other. Emotionally, the child needs both parents. So they need the encouragement to think and feel positively no matter how the parents view each other. I know this sounds harsh, but there is no more damaging act of selfishness than to place a child in a position of disowning the love he or she feels for each of the parents.

Some of you readers who are struggling to maintain your marriage for the sake of your kids will be interested to know that new research says you may be doing the right thing in staying together. There are exceptions, however. If infidelities, addictions, violence, and alcoholic behaviors are polluting the marriage pool, you may be doing the greatest service for your children by removing them from that toxicity. By doing so, you are modeling for your kids that certain behaviors are not acceptable. Boys need to learn by mother's example that men are to treat a wife with respect. Girls learn by mother's example that, at all cost, ungodly behavior will not be tolerated. Separating from ungodly behavior not only serves as a model for the kids, it rescues them from a home environment that is neither safe nor nurturing.

But let's return to this recent research that supports staying together in a low-conflict marriage. A low-conflict marriage is one in which there is no violence or destructive addiction. There is simply a loveless relationship characterized by grim-jawed determination not to divorce. Is that better for kids? It's not great, but it may be better for them than a family foundation that cracks, splits, and then falls apart.

When parents stay together, the benefit to kids is that the marriage may be "good enough" for the children even though it does not feel "good enough" for the parents. In that less than perfect relationship, the kids will still feel the security of an intact home free from the tension of "Whose house do I go to for Christmas?" and "I hate who my father married."

Another possible plus is that as the kids come to understand that no marriage, father, or mother is perfect, they witness the parents trying to provide a stable home in spite of all the imperfections. Kids learn it's possible to have conflict but still work through it well enough not to divorce. They also are witnessing the parents putting the kids' needs ahead of their own. (The realization of that selflessness will probably come only in their adulthood.)

In cases where divorce is no longer in the "maybe, maybe not" category, let's say a word about how to reduce a child's pain in the legal process. It's really a no-brainer: kids should never be dragged into a court of law, made to witness the angry exchanges of blame and hysteria between parents, and then—this is totally unthinkable—have to testify for or against Mom or Dad. All this destructively uncivilized behavior can be avoided through divorce mediation. It's not only preferable for parents and kids; it's cheaper.

Now as we wrap up this topic, let me underscore four things you probably already know but that we might just be reminded of:

1. Kids must know the divorce was not their fault.

2. Kids must be assured they will be loved by both parents.

3. Kids should never have to take sides against one parent or the other.

4. Kids should never become a substitute spouse.

Before the age of nine, most kids assume the divorce of their parents could have been prevented if they (the kids) had simply been better kids—smarter, more obedient, less self-ish, willing to consume huge servings of broccoli, or more cooperative at bedtime. The list of personal blamings is end-less. Children want to understand why daddy or mommy left and why life can't be like it used to be. It may not be appro-priate to explain all the reasons for the divorce to a child but it is important the child knows absolutely nothing they did or said caused it.

The best way to communicate that message is for the child to experience love. That's expressed not only by words but by deeds. Be available; listen; show interest in every detail of their lives; show empathy for each of the emotions they share with you. Those deeds build trust in the words "I love you."

We've emphasized the importance of never speaking negatively about the spouse, but realize that sometimes that negativity can slip in even without words—a rolling of the eyes, shrugging of the shoulders, or a massive sigh heard around the world. I know you are going to have to be a phony in some of this but do it anyway. There's a higher good.

Let's say something about how subtly and perhaps unknowingly a child can become a "spouse substitute." That can happen when the child becomes the "car" for parental pain. Confiding in the child about how much hurt, disappointment, and sadness the parent feels about the divorce is too great a burden for the child to bear. She has her own burdens about the divorce; it is the parents' job to help bear those. Once a child begins to feel responsible for making mom or dad feel better, an unhealthy role reversal has occurred.

It is not unwise to be emotionally authentic and allow the kids to see that divorce really hurts. But it is unwise for the child to feel she must somehow "fix" the parental pain by listening empathically and then trying desperately to stop the pain.

Children will grow emotionally when they see parents managing their own emotions. Parents can be models of survivor behavior. Kids can see the value of grieving the pain, managing the pain, and learn that joy truly can come in the morning. And that survival is not dependent on the kids playing the part of spouse substitute. Neither is the "joy in the morning" dependent on the kids. God ultimately provides that and invites us to remember that His ear is ever inclined toward our voices.

Life hurts us and often disappoints us. Jesus said in John 16:33, "Here on earth you will have many trials and sorrows. But take heart, because I have overcome the world." Certainly one of those trials is divorce, which produces sorrow for parents and kids. Jesus offers us hope by saying He overcame not only the sorrow of divorce but all earthly sorrow. Not that we do not experience it, but that we need not be defeated by it. Jesus is the Overcomer and He lives within us. That means we, too, are overcomers. There is then power for our personal healing and power for the healing of our kids.

My daughter, Beth, has experienced the roof cave-in of her marriage and felt the pain it produced in her life and in the lives of her two boys. This has not been easy for me to witness. Nevertheless, I've been inspired to see the overcoming power of Jesus repeatedly lead each of them from experiences of powerlessness to experiences of overcoming victory.

No amount of psychology can do what God intends to do in the lives of His Beloved. He uses and blesses psychology, divorce recovery workshops, books, and sincere efforts to make wise decisions. But in the end, our survival and victory are enabled by the indwelling Jesus who has "overcome the world."

ROOF MAINTENANCE

1. The greatest contributor to the pain of children of divorce occurs when parents openly accuse, undermine, and blame each other for all that "went

wrong." What has your experience been with this kind of parental blaming?

2. Why is it so hard on a child if he or she is forced to "choose sides" in a divorce? What are the emotional consequences for the child?

3. Do you think it is better to stay in a loveless marriage for the sake of the kids? What have your observations been about that?

4. To what degree do you think a person must place her own happiness second to the happiness of the kids? Must kids' needs always come first?

5. How do you assure the kids your divorce was not their fault?

12

DEATH:
THE ULTIMATE
CAVE-IN

An eighteenth-century man named William Palmer was hanged for poisoning his best friend. As he stepped out on the shaky gallows trap, he looked nervously at the executioner and asked, "Are you sure it's safe?" The irony of this question is not lost on us but neither is the universal fear that the question implies. Is death safe? That's an odd question. We know death is inevitable, but in what way is it either safe or unsafe?

Most people would feel safer staying on this earth. It's not a perfect place, but it is at least a known place. What we can know, see, and feel is at least familiar. Change is unsettling to most people. The most unsettling change we experience in life is death: the death of those we love and the death we know will be ours. As death brings unwanted change it also brings unwanted emotions. More often than not, those emotions don't feel safe. They cause us to feel out of control and without foundational security. Death causes us to lose our moorings and sets us adrift on a frightening sea of unfamiliarity.

Let's do a brief history about how our culture has dealt with death. Interestingly enough, the stark reality of death could not be avoided until the twentieth century. A century ago it was impossible to deny the fact of death because premature death was common. As late as 1900, the chance of a marriage lasting forty years was one in three, not because of a high divorce rate but because of early mortality. Death then typically took place in the home following a deathbed watch. Family members had to lay out, wash, and shroud the body. Viewing of the deceased took place at home, not in a funeral parlor. Death was a tangible reality that could not be denied or escaped.

In the nineteenth century the first professional undertakers established themselves as a viable alternative to the pain of tending to the bodies at home. During the Civil War, professional embalming became increasingly common and in the 1880s, cosmetic restoration of bodies became widely available. Since it was impractical to embalm and restore bodies in the deceased's home, funeral parlors began to appear at the end of the nineteenth century.

An effort to soften the pain of death was a new kind of cemetery during the early nineteenth century. The new garden cemeteries were places of tranquility where grieving relatives could find comfort in the beauty of nature. Also, the word *coffin was* replaced with *casket*, a word that meant a "jewel box."

Now in the twenty-first century, we have fewer discussions about death and dying, and as a result, far greater denial! As Woody Allen said, "I know I'm going to die. I just don't want to be there when it happens."

Jessica Mitford's book *The American Way of Death*, published in the mid 1960s, startled readers into a reevaluation of how we "do" death. Instead of the "outsourcing" of the sick and dying to sterile hospitals where care was assured by uniformed professionals carefully monitoring painkillers, the hospice movement was established. It stressed the importance of a family context for the terminally ill. A growing number of terminally ill men and women have chosen to die at home or in homelike settings known as hospices.

My husband, Ken, made that decision for himself as he realized the unwelcome cancer ravaging his body was indeed going to claim his life. He did not want to spend his remaining weeks away from home. I totally supported his desire. I put my counseling practice "on hold" and nursed him through to his final breath on May 5, 1990. He died in our bed.

I didn't do that nursing alone, however. Our kids, Jeff and Beth, popped in and out, as did many friends. That home environment was as nurturing for me as it was for Ken as he experienced his last weeks and days. Hospice care was invaluable to me as more and more medical oversight became necessary. I felt safer knowing they'd come regularly.

One afternoon, as a hospice nurse was teaching me how to monitor Ken's morphine pump, he winked at the nurse and told her his wife might try to get in on his "supply." He suggested she keep an eye on me when he no longer could. Fortunately she'd gotten used to Ken's dark humor and stopped by even when she wasn't scheduled. Her excuse was always, "I promised Ken I'd keep an eye on you."

The vigilance of the hospice support made death feel safer to me. It also felt as if I had a measure of control in the midst of foundational change. The hard reality is, whether one chooses hospice over hospital, death is not ours to control. Ultimately, when death comes, we are still set upon a sea of frightening unfamiliarity.

How then does one navigate those frightening and unfamiliar seas? One of those ways is to immerse oneself in Scripture. One of my favorite verses from Psalms is 94:19: "When my anxious thoughts multiply within me, Your consolations delight my soul" (NASB).

To those of us who have experienced the death of loved ones, "anxious thoughts" describe our near constant state of being. But that psalm takes us beyond our anxiety and points us to a solution. That solution is to remember and then ponder deeply the many consolations God provides for His Beloved. That pondering ultimately leads us from the anxiety of our soul to consolation for our soul.

We see that anxiety turn to consolation as we read of the death of Lazarus in John 11. Divine consolations were lovingly given to the deeply grieving sisters Mary and Martha. Those consolations came before the miraculous calling forth of Lazarus from the grave. What were those consolations? They were exactly the kinds we all so desperately need.

To begin with, the sisters were allowed to be real with their feelings. They fussed at Jesus. They blamed Him for not coming sooner. If He had come sooner, Lazarus would not have died. It was His fault. Jesus didn't really care enough. They were crushed.

Jesus did not chastise the sisters for their feelings. He didn't berate them for their lack of faith in Him. He simply let them talk. It is interesting Jesus did not become defensive under their accusations. He made no excuses for His delay in coming to Bethany. He simply asked them to believe in who He was and who He had always been to them.

I have experienced four major deaths of loved ones, and with each one I have fussed at God when they died. I felt personally betrayed. How could He let them die? He could have prevented it; why didn't He? Did I not pray enough . . . believe enough . . . behave well enough? Whose fault was this? If it was mine, it meant I had failed and not lived up to the standard of righteousness God required to heal my loved ones. If it was God's fault, He failed to honor His promise to hear and answer my prayers.

Both of those "fussings" are devastating, and neither brings consolation to the soul. But what we must know about our emotions is they absolutely must be released and vented. Bad feelings are composed of negative and toxic energy, which if not released, find someplace in the human body to take up lodging. For some, that is in the colon resulting in colitis. For others it may be in the back, causing ill-defined but consistent discomfort. We could add headaches, insomnia, digestive complaints, and a host of other hiding places in which our negative emotions live.

The healing point here is God receives our venting. We see that in the example of Jesus as he heard the venting of Mary and Martha. Jesus did not tell them that because they were behaving badly, they would be punished by joining Lazarus in the family tomb. Instead, what did He do? He cried with them! There was no judgment; there were tears of empathy.

Empathy provides incredible consolation. When someone actually cries with me, I know she is not only responding to the words I used in expressing my loss, but she is actually feeling my loss and entering into it with me. The consolation for the soul that has just vented it all to God is the loving, nonjudgmental extension of empathy we see Jesus offering to Mary and Martha. He honored their emotions by not only receiving their accusations but by feeling the intense loss of their brother, Lazarus.

In addition to the empathy Jesus exhibited, there may be another dimension to that empathy that extends to what each of us feels when death is experienced. John 11:33 says that as Jesus experienced the community's pain at the loss of Lazarus, He was "moved with indignation and was deeply troubled." Why was Jesus indignant? Why was He deeply troubled? Seemingly, there was no earthly reason for His troubled indignation. No one was behaving inappropriately or being disrespectful.

I believe His response was anger at death itself. He was indignant and deeply troubled not only because Lazarus died, but because we all die; we were meant to live. We were meant for a life without sorrow and disease. Our lives were to be lived without the effects of sin. But human sin brought with it human death.

Quite simply, death is an enemy. Each of us knows that whether we have framed it as such or not. We recoil from it. We are angry and indignant when it strikes. Our deepest soul knows that death is wrong, and that knowing is even deeper than the loss of our loved one. But our consolation is stated in 1 Corinthians 15:56: "For sin is the sting that results in death," but Jesus provides victory over sin and death. Death is swallowed up in victory. "O death, where is your sting?" (1 Cor. 15:55).

Jesus knew He would call Lazarus forth from the grave. He also knew that Lazarus would have to experience death all over again sometime in the future. But in the words of Isaiah 25:8, "He will swallow up death forever! The Sovereign Lord will wipe away all tears." This is a description of the work Jesus came to earth to do. But for that moment in imperfect time, Jesus was indignant and cried the tears all of us feel when the enemy strikes those we love. His example gives us permission to cry out our individual indignation. His death and victory over it give us reason to experience hope and consolation.

The story of Lazarus assures us the consolation of venting without judgment, divine empathy for human loss, and the assurance that God hears our prayers. Standing in the midst of the mourners, Jesus prays:

> "Father, thank you for hearing me. You always hear me, but I said it out loud for the sake of all these people standing here, so they will believe you sent me." (John 11:41–42)

When Jesus said, "You always hear me," He made that statement not only for the bystanders but for us standing beside our lost loved ones. We have prayed for an extension of life, and when it does not happen as we prayed, many of us wonder if God really heard our prayer. Jesus said to God, "You always hear me." We have the same degree of access to the ear of God as Jesus. God always hears our prayers. So we cannot fuss about that. What we may feel we can fuss about is why God does not do what we want Him to do.

Though that fussing may provide necessary venting, it is

ultimately counterproductive to our peace. Our greatest peace-producing truth is God's loving sovereignty. He does what He does and the timing of what He does is determined by Him. That does not mean our prayers are not invited or heard. It does not mean death is not an enemy. But God took control of the earth at the moment of creation. He will forever be in control. That means He determines the time when we are taken from this earth. There is peace in knowing God is in control of even that. Job 14:5 states, "You have decided the length of our lives. You know how many months we will live, and we are not given a minute longer." The same truth is found in Psalm 139:16: "You saw me before I was born. Every day of my life was recorded in your book. Every moment was laid out before a single day had passed."

To see the death of our loved ones as a part of God's sovereign timetable removes the sense of death as being random. God did not intend us to die; the sin choice determined that for us. But God did not lose sovereign control over the free will He allowed in the garden that resulted in the death consequence. And He has not lost control over the time any of us will leave this earth. There can be peace for our souls with the acceptance of how God has ordained the number of our days. That sovereign control also provides a sense of safety. Someone's in charge here!

When God moved me from California to Frisco, Texas, four years ago, He placed me into the midst of a phenomenal neighborhood. They are loving, kind, loyal, and tons of fun. Their fun-loving natures are expressed by monthly game nights, celebration birthday luncheons, movie expeditions, and anything that provides opportunity to socialize and laugh. My one regret in living here is I don't have time to get in on all their activity. However, I've warned them, "The day is coming."

A neighbor for whom I felt a particular kinship was named Carrie. She suffered from a rare and incurable neurological disease somewhat like Lou Gehrig's disease. The symptoms of the disease had become increasingly debilitating, but the moment we met I knew she was and always had been exceptional. She was brilliant, articulate, and possessed a sharp wit that dropped me to my knees. She, like the other neighborhood women, would drop anything to help whoever had a need. It hurt us all to see her own physical needs increase with the passing of each day. Everyone loved Carrie.

She had a deep faith in God, but at the same time, many questions about Him. The fact that her disease had taken her from a high-paying, responsible corporate position and reduced her to what she felt was a place of non productivity caused her to question her value and wonder if God truly had His hand on her life.

The two of us got together for what Carrie called "God, life, and other tidbits" whenever time allowed. Because her vocal cords were paralyzed, I had to listen intently to understand what she was saying. Her expressive eyes told me what I sometimes missed. She delighted my soul.

Last summer, after an especially rich time of sharing, I was walking her home and expressed concern about her frequent choking. I asked her what I should do if she had a violent choking spell when we were together. With typical off-handedness she said, "Just pray I don't croak." I knew the choking could be a serious consequence as her throat became increasingly paralyzed, so I promised I would pray if she promised not to "croak." She agreed and we made a commitment to get together when I returned from Denver in a few days. The very next day, after talking with her husband on the phone, Carrie hung up and apparently began choking. Because she was alone, no one knows just what happened or when, but Carrie choked to death—the very thing we all feared for her.

Had Carrie lived the number of days God had ordained for her? Yes. Was the way Carrie died also ordained for her? Of course not. God did not ordain disease or the heartbreaking consequences of disease. God hates sin. Disease and death are the by-products of sin. But in it all, God gives us assurances that His love does not fail us nor does His presence ever leave us. Carrie knows that now. The challenge is for those she left to know it as well.

The one left behind who feels the greatest loss is Carrie's mother, Bev. She is a widow and Carrie was her only child. She, too, lives down my street. Bev, like her daughter, Carrie, is utterly charming, articulate, and loves to laugh. Our hearts have broken as we see Bev, with strength and dignity, make her way through the layers of debris that showered down upon her in that catastrophic cave-in.

She is cocooned in support and love from a neighborhood that desperately wants to take away her pain. But eliminating pain is beyond human capability. What we can do is follow the example of Jesus: listen without judgment and extend empathy without restraint. But the ultimate consolation only God can provide. He defeated death on the cross and offers each of us the victory of life beyond the grave: "For every child of God defeats this evil world by trusting Christ to give the victory. And the ones who win this battle against the world are the ones who believe that Jesus is the Son of God" (1 John 5:4–5).

What is the victory of life beyond the grave? It's heaven. We will spend time on that fascinating topic in the next chapter. But another part of that victory of life beyond the grave is that we will all receive a new body. That new body will be free from pain, disease, frailty, malformation, or physical limitation of any kind. It will be what we all long for—a perfect body! Because of that I revel in the knowledge that my baby, Joanie, is free of the effects of spina bifida, Ken is free of cancer, and my parents are freed from bodies grown weak by age. I also revel in the knowledge that my friend Carrie is free of the creeping paralysis of her limbs and vital organs. She is once again enthusiastic, vibrant, and participating in all the heavenly glory swirling around her.

Let's loop back to the question I asked at the beginning of this chapter: Is death safe? We can say death can feel very unsafe. But what is safe is the God-assured promise of the celebration that is ours the moment we are reunited with those we love in a gloriously secure and perfect heaven.

ROOF MAINTENANCE

1. Have you ever fussed at God about what He did or did not do? Do you think it is wrong or unspiritual to fuss at Him?

2. Does it make sense to you that Jesus was angry about death in John 11:33? Is that a new thought to you? Do you have a right to be angry about death?

3. What is the difference between being angry at God about death and being angry about death itself? Why is it important to know the difference?

4. Do you think death is an enemy?

5. How does knowing that God has a sovereign timetable for each of us bring comfort? Do you think Job 14:5 means exactly what it says: "You have decided the length of our lives. You know how many months we will live, and we are not given a minute longer"?

13

HEAVEN:
NO MORE CAVE-INS

Living in stressful times causes most of us to long for heaven. Scripture promises it to be a place without stress—a place where there is total perfection, an environment free of all soul pollution. One of the greatest soul pollutants this side of heaven is, of course, stress. As we all know, stress accompanies cave-ins.

Let's take a minute to take a quasi-serious, but slightly playful, look at how people continuously search for what heaven promises: stress-free living. That search has produced various suggestions for ways in which earth-bound persons can alleviate stress.

We understand that stress creeps; it does its work slowly, damaging the body's organs in much the same way alcohol and cigarettes do. As the father of research, Hans Selve once wrote, "It's not stress that kills us; it's our reaction to it." So then, if we manage our thoughts and emotions more successfully, our reaction to stress will not be as intense. That's an encouraging suggestion. We know Scripture supports the renewing of our minds by thinking on "whatsoever things are good and lovely" (Phil. 4:8 KJV).

I recently read another stress-reliever study that suggests that touch in the form of massage, hugging, and kissing decreases stress hormones by increasing the feel-good hormone oxytocin in the body. This touch therapy also lowers blood pressure. You have to admit, that's an appealing suggestion.

If, however, grabbing persons in a warm embrace with an accompanying kiss creates unwelcome consequences, here's another way to experience touch. Perhaps you've heard about those fish pedicures, where tiny, toothless fish eat the dead skin off your feet. This is an ancient Asian tradition where one places the feet on smooth rocks in a blue-bottom bowl. The fish then dash about eagerly nibbling on your toes and heels.

There are two types of fish in the bowl: *chin chin* from China and *garra rufa* from Turkey. The chin chin eat the dead skin, while the garra rufa inject an enzyme called dithranol to promote healthy skin growth.

Several weeks ago I witnessed the stress-lowering fish pedicure while I was getting my nails done. Four women had driven some distance just so they could be nibbled and injected by tiny fish. They squealed, giggled, and clapped saying it tickled, while another said it felt soothing.

They recognized me as a speaker with Women of Faith and insisted I have the fish pedicure. One of the women splashed out to pay for my pedicure, so I felt obligated then to drop my feet onto the smooth stones and endure the ravenous enthusiasm of the "toothless fish." I don't know if it was the determination of the Turkish garra rufa to inject me with dithranol or the relentless nibbling of the little Chinese chin chin, but my stress level shot up to stroke level. I tried to disguise my horror, but it wasn't until I got home, had a cup of tea, and read Scripture that I regained pre-pedicure peace.

Actually there is no greater stress reliever than the Word of God. It speaks to every worry and reminds us God is in control of all things. Try munching on this stress-relieving verse: I guarantee the results.

> Above the floodwaters is GOD's throne
>> from which his power flows,
>> from which he rules the world.
> GOD makes his people strong.
> GOD gives his people peace. (Ps. 29:10–11 MSG)

I love the words "God rules the world" and in so doing "makes his people strong." There is no doubt that truth provides foundational security for our souls and minds as we experience the various cave-ins of life. (The fish pedicure does not qualify as a cave-in, though it came close.)

But there is another tremendously effective stress reliever many of us fail to consider. In fact, the value of that stress reliever is frequently overlooked and rarely even thought about. What is it? It's the contemplation of heaven!

You may be thinking, *How does contemplating heaven lower my stress? Beyond being grateful that there is a heaven, what is there to contemplate?* Colossians 3:1–2 provides a godly word for us regarding heaven-contemplations: "Set your sights on the realities of heaven, where Christ sits at God's right hand in the place of honor and power. Let heaven fill your thoughts. Do not think about things down here on earth."

In the words of my grandson, "Fat chance on that one!" We can't imagine thinking more about heaven than earth. We are up to our eyeballs with "earth stuff." Not only that, we may think we don't know enough about heaven to find thinking about it stress reducing.

I think that perfectly defines our reticence about heaven contemplation. We don't really know enough about it. Once again I'll quote my grandson. When I asked him what he thought heaven would be like, he paused a long time and then said, "Well, I don't want to hurt your feelings, Maunga, but I think it might be boring. There's probably tea for you but I'll bet there are no Skittles." For many people, the most attractive thing about heaven is we won't take any of our stress with us. That is very appealing. But after the stress relief, what do we do there? Is there a chance it might be boring? Perhaps we need to know a lot more about heaven.

The first thing we need to know about heaven is not news to those of us well schooled in Scripture. We will finally see and experience the actual presence of God the Creator and of Jesus our Savior. Quite frankly, I cannot wrap my mind around that ultimate encounter. There have been many times when the extremity of my circumstances and the stress resulting from them have created within me an intense longing to see, actually see, Jesus. There is no doubt that to know, feel, and see His tangible presence would bring relief and release from my stress. But in addition to the comfort of His encouraging presence, I am also just plain curious! What does He actually look like? Does He have dark brown eyes with long eyelashes like so many Middle Eastern men? Will He have a slight body frame or a strong, muscular physique? Now those aren't questions I wonder about concerning the look of God. I can't imagine the physical proportion of the One who flung the stars and moons into place; He who "rules the world" is beyond my ability to envision.

The point is, whatever our images may be, we are going to actually see the Ones who gave us life and who will welcome us with a love beyond our wildest imaginings. I just got goose bumps writing that!

As we discussed in the chapter on death, we know our loved ones, if they are believers, will one day stand with us as we become citizens of heaven. The apostle Paul wrote encouraging words on the topic in 1 Thessalonians 4:13–14:

And now, brothers and sisters, I want you to know what will happen to the Christians who have died so you will not be full of sorrow like people who have no hope. For since we believe that Jesus died and was raised to life again, we also believe that when Jesus comes, God will bring back with Jesus all the Christians who have died.

When our loved ones die we experience the loss of a continued earthly relationship. But that relationship is not truly lost; it is only interrupted. We will join them in the perfection of all that heaven is. That is stress-relieving encouragement.

But now let's consider some thoughts about heaven that may be new contemplations to you. Many of them are new to me. I am indebted to the research and insights of Randy Alcorn's excellent book *Heaven* as well as Albert M. Wolters's book *Creation Regained* in sharing these new thoughts.

Let's refamiliarize ourselves with some key verses about God's plan for creating a new heaven and a new earth:

Behold, I will create new heavens and a new earth.

(Isaiah 65:17 NIV)

As the new heavens and the new earth that I make will endure before me,' declares the LORD, 'so will your name and descendants endure.

(Isaiah 66:22 NIV)

But in keeping with his promise we are looking forward to a
new heaven and a new earth, the home of righteousness.

(2 Peter 3:13 NIV)

Then I saw a new heaven and a new earth, for the first heaven
and the first earth had passed away.

(Revelation 21:1 NIV)

So what do these verses mean? What is the point of God
creating a new heaven and a new earth? I've generally assumed
that because the sin-choice in Eden messed things up so
badly, God would ultimately wash His hands of it all and start
over. Here's the new contemplation. When God created the
heavens and the earth, He called them "very good." God is
not going to wash His hands of it all; He's going to restore it
all. Randy Alcorn's biblical research suggests we won't go to
heaven and leave earth behind. Instead, God will bring heaven
and earth together into the same dimension. Ephesians 1:10
says that God's perfect plan is "to bring all things in heaven
and on earth together under one head, even Christ" (NIV).

What fascinates me is that the "new earth" is actually our
present earth but a fully restored earth . . . an earth without
rabbits destroying my flowers, smog enveloping my city, or
humidity creating mold in my walls. It is the earth as God

originally intended it to be. He has never given up on his original creation. It will once again be a perfect earth as it was before the Fall:

In the words of Albert Wolters in *Creation Regained*:

. . . Theologians have sometimes spoken of salvation as 're-creation', not to imply that God scraps his earlier creation and in Jesus Christ makes a new one, but rather to suggest that he hangs on to his fallen original creation and salvages it. He refuses to abandon the works of his hands . . . in fact he sacrifices his own Son to save his original project. Humankind, which has botched its original mandate and the whole creation along with it, is given another chance in Christ; we are reinstated as God's managers on earth. The original good creation is to be restored.

God's intent is to finish what He started. What He started was a sinless world in which total harmony was experienced at all levels of existence: plant, animal, human. A curse fell upon that sinless world when Satan convinced Adam and Eve to disobey God. When they joined ranks with evil, God never lost His earth. Psalm 24:1 says, "The earth is the LORD's, and everything in it, the world, and all who live in it" (NIV).

God began the reclaiming of His world by offering salvation

to His people through Jesus. Salvation provides cleansing and forgiveness from the curse of sin. But that's not the only item on the divine agenda. First John 3:8 says the reason the Son of God appeared was to destroy the devil's work. God's destruction of the devil's work will be complete when the curse is lifted from the earth.

Revelation 21:1 says the old earth will pass away. But it will experience a resurrection. It will no longer be cursed; it will become the new perfect earth. Evil will be destroyed and heaven on earth will be established. In Randy Alcorn's words in *50 Days of Heaven*:

> God's stated purpose for us is to rule the earth forever as His children and heirs. Christ's mission was and is to redeem what was lost in the Fall and to destroy all competitors to God's dominion, authority, and power. When everything is put under his feet and mankind rules the earth as kings under the King of kings, everything at last will be as God intends. This peculiar era of rebellion will be over forever. At last, all God's people and the redeemed universe itself will bask in the joy of our Master.

Wow! What amazing new contemplation these thoughts provide.

These contemplations also assure us it is not wrong to love all the good parts of our present earth. The grandeur of the Rocky Mountains, the Columbia River Gorge with its multiple cascading waterfalls, the sweet pastoral quiet of rural meadows and valleys—the never-ending drama of magnificent beauty spots is endless. God does not waste anything; He will simply return it all to its original splendor for our eternal pleasure. There is no way such a heaven on earth will ever be boring.

Another fascinating contemplation is to consider what kind of body we will have as we walk about this new earth. We learn a lot about our resurrection bodies as we read about Jesus and His resurrection body. First John 3:2 says our bodies will be like His: "But we do know that when [Jesus] comes we will be like him." Philippians 3:20 says that the Lord Jesus will transform our lowly bodies so they will be like His glorious body.

We know that the body of Jesus, when He walked away from the tomb, was recognizable as the body that died on the cross. He said to His disciples after His resurrection, "It is I myself!" (Luke 24:39 NIV); the stunned disciples saw the marks of the crucifixion on His body. A resurrected body does not mean a new body is created; if that were the case, the old body would have remained in the tomb with crucifixion scars.

The body of Jesus was resurrected. He walked the earth in His resurrected body for forty days. He walked and talked with two disciples on the road to Emmaus. He cooked breakfast for His disciples one morning on the seashore. He also suddenly appeared in a locked room where the disciples were gathered. They touched Him, questioned Him, and Jesus answered them.

We, too, will have resurrection bodies that are recognizable. They will be transformed but the original will not be eliminated. We will remain the unique beings that God originally created but no longer will be weakened by disease, disability, or deformity. Our bodies will rise to the level of perfection.

My little grandson, who assured me I would have tea in heaven but that he would probably not have Skittles and might possibly find heaven boring, expressed a common fear that heaven must be dull. The question asked is, "What is there to do?" If you have shown little aptitude for harp-strumming, might your expectations be reduced to nothing more than a vague hope for good food? There are many misconceptions about what we will experience in heaven, and the major one is that heaven will be boring. Where on earth did that rumor get started? If we find perfect beauty, perfect relatedness, expressions of perfect love, perfect physical health, perfect mental health, perfect family reunions, perfectly well-behaved children, perfect cocker spaniels who never tinkle on the carpet, zero stress about anything and everything—if that sounds boring, you might want to grab a bag of Skittles while you know where to find them!

Now here's another totally nonboring heaven contemplation: there will indeed be perfect food and drink. Its purpose is to celebrate all that is heavenly and divinely restored. The food is not designed to nourish bodies that will grow weak from hunger. It is instead another perfecting of what God means for His Beloved to enjoy. God puts a high value on the simple act of eating. Words for "eating," "meals," and "food" appear more than one thousand times in Scripture. The word translated "feast" occurs 187 times. Eating is celebrating. It's getting together with those we love to laugh, talk, and revel in heavenly food and drink. Luke 14:15 says, "Blessed is the man who will eat at the feast in the kingdom of God" (NIV).

There are specifically referenced feasts we are told about in Scripture to which we are invited! Check out these future celebrations:

In Jerusalem, the LORD Almighty will spread a wonderful feast for everyone around the world. It will be a delicious feast of good food with clear, well-aged wine and choice beef.

(Isaiah 25:6)

Then he took a cup of wine, and when he had given thanks for it, he said, "Take this and share it among yourselves. For I will not drink wine again until the Kingdom of God has come."

(Luke 22:17–18)

Culminating the feast of all feasts is the wedding feast of the Lamb. We are the bride. The groom is our husband—God. Revelation 19:6–7 describes that monumental celebration with these words:

Then I heard again what sounded like the shout of a huge crowd, or the roar of mighty ocean waves, or the crash of loud thunder: 'Hallelujah! For the Lord our God, the Almighty, reigns. Let us be glad and rejoice and honor him. For the time has come for the wedding feast of the Lamb, and his bride has prepared herself.

So then, let's now review what it is possible to know about heaven. To begin with, we know it is a place where we, God's Bride, will luxuriate in His presence for all eternity. We know it is a place where there will be no stress, sadness, or sickness. We know we will have perfect and transformed new bodies like the "glorious body" of Christ.

We know God is the Redeemer and makes all things new.

Not only does He redeem our souls and bodies, He intends to redeem all creation that was blighted and ruined by the Fall. He will make a new heaven and new earth over which He will reign for all time. No matter how successfully we pull away from the stress of earth and contemplate the perfection of heaven, God says this about our contemplations: "No eye has seen, no ear has heard, and no mind has imagined what God has prepared for those who love him" (1 Cor. 2:9).

Perhaps our greatest stress reliever as we contemplate heaven is simply this: there will be no more cave-ins! What we will have instead is so fantastic, so far beyond our ability to imagine, that we simply wait in anticipation for what God will one day present to us. Because we know His style, it will be worth the wait!

ROOF MAINTENANCE

1. Do you look forward to heaven primarily because you will leave all your stresses behind you? Do you ever feel guilty that your wish for heaven is more about "getting out of here" than meeting God?

2. Do you have any images of how you expect Jesus to look when you see Him? How about God? What are your expectations?

3. Have you ever worried that maybe heaven might be boring? If so, what have your images of heaven been? What kinds of things have you thought would go on there?

4. How do you respond to the teaching that our present earth will be restored to its original state of perfection? Does that seem weird to you? Why or why not?

5. Discuss what you learned about your resurrected body as you considered the resurrected body of Jesus. How is this knowledge a comfort to you?

AFTERWORD

As we have talked about our various roof cave-ins throughout this book, let me say again we always need to be
aware of the construction of our roof. The construction of the
roof is composed of what we think, what we believe, and what
we do about what we think and believe regarding the cave-in.

I also suggested there may be an out-of-the-box solution
to a cave-in, something that doesn't make sense and would
not naturally occur to us. So then, I'm going to suggest one
of those "out-of-the-boxers" and admit that though I try to
use it, I don't always do it well.

Thank God for your cave-in. Thank Him for every aspect of it:

that it happened, the way it happened, and the resulting debris you're buried in. (I told you it made no sense.) This thank-you solution is stated in *The Message* translation of Psalm 100. Read the psalm here and watch for the solution phrase.

> On your feet now—applaud GOD!
>> Bring a gift of laughter,
>>> sing yourselves into his presence. . . .
>
> Enter with the password: Thank you!
>> Make yourselves at home, talking praise.
>>> Thank him. Worship him. (vv. 1–2, 4)

"Thank you" is our password; praise and worship become our behavior. That does not mean we don't grieve or vent our feelings. It means simply we conclude each prayer with praise and a thank-you not just for His promise of a continual presence within us buoying us up and encouraging our healing, but also a specific thank-you for the cave-in itself.

You don't need to search for all the ways God is going to ultimately turn your cave-in to an "all things work together for good." Simply thank Him specifically for your cave-in. You can do this a gazillion times a day, saying, "Thank You

Jesus, for . . ." You are not living in denial because you are feeling your pain, venting your pain, and grieving your pain. But after your healthy venting, you conclude by using the password "Thank You."

WOMEN OF FAITH®

Women of Faith, North America's largest women's conference, is an experience like no other. Thousands of women — all ages, sizes, and backgrounds — come together in arenas for a weekend of love and laughter, stories and encouragement, drama, music, and more. The message is simple. The result is life-changing.

What this conference did for me was to show me how to celebrate being a woman, mother, daughter, grandmother, sister or friend.
— Anne, Corona, CA

I appreciate how genuine each speaker was and that they were open and honest about stories in their life   even the difficult ones.
— Amy, Fort Worth, TX

GO, you MUST go. The Women of Faith team is wonderful, uplifting, funny, blessed. Don t miss out on a chance to have your life changed by this incredible experience.
— Susan, Hartford, CT